WHITMAN COLLEGE LIBRARY

P9-DVH-385

LIBRARY

COMMON
CULTURE
AND
THE
GREAT
TRADITION

Mayor J. W. Houghawout seemed to enjoy his role in the tiny nineteenth-century village of Lexington, Virginia. (So did his dogs.) He had many links not only to the land and the people, but to the common past. An insatiable hunter, he often startled the citizenry by sounding his hunting horn at dawn from Court House Square. Thus did he perpetuate an ancient ritual. (Photograph: Courtesy of the author.)

WHITMAN COLLEGE LIBRARY Withdrawn by
Whitman College Library

COMMON CULTURE AND THE GREAT TRADITION

The Case for Renewal

MARSHALL W. FISHWICK

CONTRIBUTIONS TO THE STUDY OF POPULAR CULTURE,
——————————————————————————NUMBER 2

GREENWOOD PRESS
Westport, Connecticut • London, England

E
169.1
.F544
1982

PENROSE MEMORIAL LIBRARY
WHITMAN COLLEGE
WALLA WALLA. WASHINGTON 99362

Library of Congress Cataloging in Publication Data

Fishwick, Marshall William.
  Common culture and the great tradition.

  (Contributions to the study of popular culture,
ISSN 0198-9871 ; no. 2)
  Bibliography: p.
  Includes index.
  1. United States—Popular culture. 2. Popular cul-
ture. I. Title. II. Series: Contributions in the
study of popular culture ; no. 2
  E169.1.F544   973   81-4232
  ISBN 0-313-23042-0 (lib. bdg.)   AACR2

Copyright © 1982 by Marshall W. Fishwick

All rights reserved. No portion of this book may be
reproduced, by any process or technique, without the
express written consent of the publisher.

Library of Congress Catalog Card Number: 81-4232
ISBN: 0-313-23042-0
ISSN: 0198-9871

First published in 1982

Greenwood Press
A division of Congressional Information Service, Inc.
88 Post Road West, Westport, Connecticut 06881

Printed in the United States of America

10 9 8 7 6 5 4 3 2 1

PENROSE MEMORIAL LIBRARY
RECEIVED

DEC 10 1987
88- 3280
ACQUISITIONS DEP'T

For Tom Barrett, Marion Junkin, and Frank Gillam:
Ah Yes, I Remember Them Well . . .

"We are all linked with one another in a common chain."

Cicero

"Art thou base, common and popular?"

William Shakespeare

"The past is never dead, it's not even past."

William Faulkner

CONTENTS

COMMON
CULTURE
AND
THE
GREAT
TRADITION

1
A COMMONPLACE INTRODUCTION

We have much in common. That, in five words, is my central theme. I even have something in common with Captain Ahab: both of us sought and found the great white whale.

Captain Ahab, hero of Herman Melville's epical nineteenth-century novel *Moby Dick*, girdled the globe seeking his whale. I merely went to a railroad siding to see mine, near my home in Roanoke, Virginia.

The whale I sought had been washed ashore, salvaged, and bought by some descendant of P. T. Barnum. On the canvas mural stretched around the flatcar, the dead beast was shown swallowing and spitting out ships like peanut shells. A lad of six, I found it awe inspiring. For ten cents—the barker preferred "one tenth of a dollar"—you could walk up a wooden ramp, go behind the canvas, and confront Leviathan for yourself.

The word spread and crowds flocked in. The fast-talking promotor anticipated a bucketful of coins before carting his odorous yet wondrous treasure off to blubberland. Even the local preacher stopped by (but demanded free entry—benefit of clergy). He was inspired enough to recall a line from Psalm 104: "There go the ships, and there is that leviathan, whom Thou hast made to take his pastime therein."

Clutching a dime in my palm-sweaty hand, I walked up the ramp, plunked down my dime, and entered. There he was! Look! Staring right at me with glassy eyes set above a massive mouth. For an instant, I was afraid to move.

I remember that instant, that day, that whale. Very little from my early childhood is as vivid: how many times has that monster invaded my dreams? There was something primordial about the episode. The boy and the beast—we were down to rock bottom. We were at the level that I shall call, in the chapters ahead, common culture.

The years that followed were largely spent mastering elite culture and winning a trade-title (professor) that would set me apart from common clay. What I am about to write now might be called *Confessions of an Ex-Elitist*.

Coming from "the right side of the tracks," enjoying "better" people and "superior" schools, I went without question to *the* university, then on to Ivy U. Unconsciously, I donned the robes of Platonism—that haute couture of Academia. Exposed to "the best that has been thought and said" (no one ever questioned who decided, and indeed who chose), I joined a Greek-letter fraternity. "The others" were openly dubbed "barbarians." Intent on the True and the Beautiful, I read less and less literature and more and more criticism. That took me ever higher in Higher Education. Up up I went, until

> Established in his eminence of taste
> This little man has little time to waste;
> And so the only books at which he looks
> Are books on books, or books on books on books.

In self-defense, I can claim that, unlike Pooh-Bah, I was not born sneering. But like Gilbert and Sullivan's famous snob, once begun I found it easy. English instructors who sneered at American literature but read T. S. Eliot (an expatriate) by candle-light increased my elitist bent. Other acceptable labels were purist, highbrow, cognoscente, sophisticated, educated. Onward and upward to a Ph.D. and a spot on that icon of icons, the Academic Ladder.

Steeped in Plato, I turned my back on Parmenides, who thought the time would come when philosophy would not despise even the meanest things, even those of which the mention provokes a smile. About face. Parmenides, take me, a late bloomer. Do for me what you can.

My blooming came in the 1960s. Like many academics living through tempestous days, I was forced to rethink the meaning of radical. The origin of that much-abused word is *radix*, or root. The radical tries to get back to his roots, to seek out the original and fundamental things. In so doing, I came upon common culture and the great tradition.

That meant examining my own grass roots and those from which America springs. The term itself, which the dictionary calls "U.S. colloquial," means close to, or emerging spontaneously from, the people. Isn't that the place to look for roots?

Here the principles of Parmenides have not been ignored. The concrete is chosen over the abstract and the "meanest things" are not despised. Intuition and emotional attachment rate higher than rational analysis; intellectual fads are ignored. Here one finds, Conal Furay notes in *The Grass-Roots Mind in America*, "a mind of staid judgment but easy credulity, that moves not in the intellectual's fashion of idea to idea but of thing to thing." Such thinking does not draw from the metaphysical or existential. It posits a knowable, workable world in which people live hour by hour, day by day, showing a basic composure in the face of the wrenching influences of the twentieth century.

Little thought goes to the Ortega y Gassets who see "the masses" destroying "art." Few are impressed with T. S. Eliot's *Definition of Culture* or Ezra Pound's fascination with obscure ideograms. Instead, the grass-roots mind, guardian of the common culture, seeks the direct and the particular and a personalization of whatever is experienced. I have come, in my life, to find this approach sensible and refreshing.

My respect for the complex thought-systems and speculations of our electrifying century—and those who have documented and criticized it—is profound. I have been blessed with great teachers, like James Southall Wilson, Peters Rushton, Rene Wellek, Cleanth Brooks, Robert Penn Warren, Stanley Williams, and Arnold Toynbee. With such minds, high culture reaches impressive peaks. But I have come to feel that one cheats himself, as a human being, if he does not know what is being said and done in the valleys.

Chapters herein try to interpret a human story that goes back not generations and centuries, but millennia. I try to establish the early triumph of common culture, its shattering and splintering in the modern world, and its metamorphosis in our own electronic revolutionary century. Such a thesis cannot be "proven" in a modest volume—or in many weighty tomes. I seek merely a new framework, or outline for further examination.

What I do not seek or relish is yet another skirmish with those perennial knights who engage in the War of Words. I agree with Benjamin DeMott, who thinks that endless dickering over levels and terms of culture has become counterproductive; and with Abraham Kaplan, who holds that unremitting talk about "the good" is not only boring but also usually inconsequential:

> Aesthetic theory that is preoccupied with artistic virtue is largely irrelevant both to artistic experience and to critical practice, confronted as they are with so much vice.[1]

At a time when "back to basics" has become a battle cry, I try to discover what is basic, or common, in our culture. Proclaiming something "in," popular, or new is old hat. Historians know that every generation has the New Look, the New Deal, and the New Frontier. The ancient Hebrews and Greeks observed that there is nothing new under the sun; that Whirl is king; that much change and ferment are illusory. Even the term "culture" is relatively new. In *To Hell with Culture*, Herbert Read says he has been unable to find any use of the term before 1510.

Major scholarship in mass media and common culture began

to appear in the 1950s. In America, it was dominated by the empiral method—especially that of Harold Laswell, whose dictum "Who says what in which channel, to whom, with what effect?" became cultic. Europeans opened other channels. In 1957, Martin Grotjahn viewed the arts through the framework of Sigmund Freud and sexual pathology. Three years later, English critic Raymond Williams' Marxist-oriented study, *The Long Revolution*, updated the work of V. I. Lenin's comrade Georgi Plekhanov, the first Marxist to write fully about popular culture. Plekhanov's influence has been enormous, not only in the Soviet Union, but also throughout the world. Edgar Morin interpreted popular culture through the marketplace, Claude Lévi-Strauss through structural linguistics, and Roland Barthes through semiology.[2] Barthes' *Systeme de la Mode* (1967) was the best received European interpretation of the decade. Two years later, in America, Morse Peckham found pornography the key to a new theoretical understanding, in *Art and Pornography*.[3] But the continuing hold of quantitative studies and empirical research dominated most research in the United States.

"Popular" culture became a recognizable academic "movement" in the 1960s and acquired the requisite pattern of journal, central office, and annual convention. It was seen, optimistically, as a point of convergence for humanities and social sciences. The emerging "field" was to be pragmatic. "What works best is the best methodology."

The new Popular Culture Association served scholars by providing a way of incorporating what others considered a "vast ooze of the mass mind" from folk festivals to movies, comics, and sports as legitimate subjects of study. Students were attracted to subjects made "relevant" by the focus on their own world as teachers applied such tools as icon, genre, and motif to the range of popular phenomena. The movement challenged the "new critical" orientation that was dominant in much of the humanities. Since popular objects were shaped by market forces in their inspiration, production, distribution, and consumption, it was hard to hold to the "new criticism dogma" that the work itself as read, seen, or heard in the abstract was the only legitimate subject. The popular culture orientation put the artifacts in social context and challenged the assumption that intellectual discourse could take place abstracted from life.

Ultimately, what is involved is the democratizing of scholarship. No one said this would be easy: many think it impossible. Those intellectual aristocrats, who thought so much and so well, managed for centuries when the connection between their thoughts and the sources of power was direct. When those trained by the church chose popes, and those who wore the Old School Tie ran cabinet, college and empire, elite methods worked. That day has passed.

A combination of factors still not fully understood is responsible: technology, ideology, and mobility. In the years from Theodore Roosevelt to Ronald Reagan, the United States shifted from mass industrial to information society. The impact was even more profound than the nineteenth-century move from an agricultural to an industrial society. Farmer to laborer to clerk— the best short formula for understanding America.

In the very years during which American Studies was coming into being, the society it was studying was undergoing a sea change. In 1950, 65 percent of working people were in the industrial sector; by 1980, that figure had shrunk to 30 percent. At the same time, the number in the information occupations rose from 17 to 50 percent and was accelerating. Instead of capital, knowledge and data had become the chief strategic resources. This meant a basic restructuring of the work environment, even of the physical environment. Books like E. F. Schumacher's *Small Is Beautiful* assaulted head-on one of the most sacred American platitudes—bigger is better. Talk of intermediate technology, appropriate technology, and appropriate scale changed the whole focus of American mythology.

In the second half of the twentieth century—for the first time in American history—decentralization was stronger than centralization. Individual and ethnic diversity became major themes, as we gave up the myth of the melting pot. Black became beautiful, and everyone was encouraged to "do your own thing." Perceiving this, popular culture courses began to explore and extol the multiple option society. By 1980, a survey by the prestigious *Chronicle of Higher Education* revealed that more than 1 million students were enrolled in almost 20,000 "popular culture courses" at American colleges and universities.

Included were many courses in ethnic studies, women's studies, media, sports, regionalism, and science fiction. Sometimes two or more of these trends coalesced. Women science fiction writers, for example, became a separate genre, featuring books like Ursula Le Guin's *The Dispossessed* (1974), Marge Piercy's *Women on the Edge of Time* (1976), and Suzy McKee Charnas' *Motherlines* (1979).

On the world scene, Marxist studies and scholarship made equally dramatic shifts and advances. In these years, Marxism became a moving force in hundreds of millions of lives. The power of a rifle is not lessened if the man wielding it is not properly educated or dressed. There is no way of segregating the electronic beeps that have turned the atmosphere into a source of constant information.

Even the word "revolution" does not and never will again mean what it meant when rocks, guns, and bombs could decide issues. Not only on the battlefield, but in the media, will the battles for men's minds be won or lost. But media history is as long as military history. To understand, we must not only look around; we must look back.

For more centuries than we can number, Traditional Man believed in mysteries he could not fathom. The repetition of archetypal gestures dramatized this; their truth he never questioned. He loved carnivals with their clowns, charlatans, and mountebanks. Fairy tales were a constant and common delight. The Ugly Duckling, Snow White, and local saints were as real to him as his parents or neighbors. They were timeless because they participated in a transcendent reality.

The Now is so vivid, so compelling, that we have not seen how much of our new wine comes in old bottles. The shrewd French social philosopher Comte Saint-Simon (1760-1825) observed that while experiencing many contradictory political and social systems he learned that consistent, deeply rooted social tendencies were impervious to change. In our own time, historian Louis B. Wright suggests:

> If it is desirable to trace the pedigree of modern America's popular culture, we shall find most of its ideology implicit in the

middle-class thought of Elizabethan England. The historian of American culture must look back to the Renaissance and read widely in the forgotten literature of tradesmen.[4]

Indeed, other historians insist that we must look back much farther than that. Two examples are Slicher Van Bath's *Agrarian History of Western Europe A.D. 500-1850* (1963) and Robert Trow-Smith's *Life from the Land: The Growth of Farming in Western Europe* (1967). We need to know much more about preindustrial family structure, leisure, work, and play. There has been a constant tendency to idealize the past, but many who retain a nostalgia for the countryside never go back to the plow or pail. The work of such English scholars as J. H. Hexter and Peter Laslett and the formation in 1964 of the Cambridge Group for the History of Population and Social Structure have provided our most accurate picture yet of preindustrial Europe.

One is struck, these scholars point out, with the tiny scale of life in early times, especially of the small size of the group in which nearly everybody spent their entire lives. There were few hotels, hostels, apartments for single persons; fewer hospitals; and almost no young men and women living on their own. In this landscape of meadows and open fields, with village communities scattered among them, there were many groups but only one basic mythic interpretation of life. And (if one defines "class" as a number of people banded together in the exercise of collective power) there was only one class . . . only one body of persons capable of concerted action over the whole area of society. The head of the poorest family was the head of *something*. Workers did not form a million *outs* facing a few *ins*. They were not in a *mass* situation. England was a large rural hinterland, attached to a vast metropolis through a network of insignificant local centers.[5]

There was still a bit of that world left in my English grandfather, William Cross, who told me about his own youth, games, and holidays. A mechanic who loved his tools, he measured achievement by the strength and skill of his hands. He moved from the little town of Wincobank to the New World, but he brought the Old World with him. In so doing, he became one of my major links to common culture.

Laslett goes on to explore, in that preindustrial world, births, marriages, and deaths; personal discipline and social structure; social structure and revolution; the pattern of authority with its vast complexities. What was it like, he muses, to live an entirely oral life? In a world dominated by reading and writing, to face crises without the institutional patterns and supports we have come to take for granted? With few records or opinions, it is hard to be certain how they viewed their own lives. Scholars of popular culture today confront the task of building an adequate foundation on premodern material and assumptions.

Most of these scholars think of mass culture as the product of recent mass production and distribution. Some conceive of it more narrowly yet, as media entertainment. Recently, a few have begun to challenge this approach, and to explore popular culture before printing. There is, they think, a whole body of important material that has been ignored or misinterpreted.

A leader of this new school, Fred E. H. Schroeder, tells how he came to challenge the accepted parameters. In a Chicago museum, Schroeder examined small figurines that the Egyptians mass produced for funerals and communal worship. Later, he discovered similar molds from Tibet. Now he had a technological connection to Sony radios, Coke bottles, the Bay Psalm Book, and the Gutenberg Bible. He had discovered ancient popular culture.[6]

Schroeder's work, and that of others, cautions us against cultural provincialism, timid scholarship, and twentieth-centuryism. In discovering the common culture of the remote past, we come closer to discovering and understanding ourselves. Historic connections and precedents, especially folk and ethnic culture, are crucial. Without knowing what was popular yesterday, and why, we can never hope to understand what is popular today.

Even if we have yet to develop a *method* of studying (or even classifying) common culture, we have at least discovered some concepts that serve us well. One concept is *formula*, which allows us to analyze the conventions and inventions used in the popular arts and to devise new categories and meanings. Putting together a "popular" novel, song, play, or mystery is like baking a cake: good cooks know the ingredients and how to mix them.

Ingredients (or conventions) include characters, myths, settings, rituals, and artifacts. These items make popular culture predictable. The inventions (elements that are innovative) add just enough of the new to attract the audience. Minor variations from the norm introduce new ideas and adjust us to change. Hence, the form moves forward, not at the pace of the hare, but at the pace of the tortoise.

Who suggests the changes, sponsors the invention, juggles the formulas? No one is certain; but they seem to be like the puppeteers who are out of sight when they pull the strings. Or should we call them manipulators who know when the time has come and can orchestrate variation and change to suit their own needs and inventiveness?

Such manipulators might be publicists, advertisers, agents, producers, artists, writers. The pioneer studies about such people are only beginning to appear. In 1969, Bruce A. Lohof published his essay on "The Higher Meaning of Marlboro Cigarettes" and called our attention to the complex process by which "The Marlboro Man" was invented. He used material from trade journals (like *Advertising Age* and *Editor and Publisher*) and allowed us to see how the work of one man (Leo Burnett) set the myth in motion. The "making" of the Beatles, and many other rock groups, has occupied able young scholars. But their work is monographic rather than comprehensive. They dig a single well and never venture into the question of oil production.

Seldom do they get to that special place between reality and fantasy where things have meaning beyond those immediately suggested by the senses. Play, life-styles, customs, comics, fads, movements—here one needs to study the natural flow of experience and nonverbal language. We get brilliant insights in Edward T. Hall's *The Hidden Dimension*, Martha Davis' *Understanding Body Movement*, and Claude Lévi-Strauss' various articles on the structural study of myth—but this is not a full "methodology."

Is "method" what we need? Is not the real meaning of culture *outside* any precise method, tied in to the understanding of the erratic and irrational world that people inhabit and relish?[7]

Rather than adapting a method, we might instead cleanse ourselves of pompous abstractions and methodological clichés. Too often we assume that if we remove the shirt of a wealthy man we'll find Robber Baron tattooed on his chest. Not so.

For over forty years, American Studies (the parent-discipline for Popular Culture) has been debating whether it is a discipline and whether it can develop a method. This has been not only unproductive but counterproductive; a kind of highbrow narcissism that we like to decry in the medieval scholastics. If we keep asking, as did T. S. Eliot's Prufrock, how we can begin, how we can presume, we'll *never* get far down the road.

Some have struggled, with modest success, to classify culture critics, if not the subject matter itself. In 1957, Harold Rosenberg gave them political labels, ranging from *arch conservatives* to *radicals*. Stuart Hall, in 1964, proposed four categories: providers, traditionalists, progressives, and radicals. Russel Nye's terms (1970) were elitists, optimists, and revisionists. Horace Newcomb (1974) divided positions into visionaries, social scientists, culture critics, and popular arts analysts. many other schemes emerged, but these received the widest attention and support.

Michael Real addressed the problem in 1977, when he published *Mass-Mediated Culture.* He placed six points on a continuum, ranging from complete acceptance of popular culture on one end to absolute rejection on the other.

1. Liberal Apologists
2. Historical Objectivists
3. Progressive Elitists
4. Traditional Elitists
5. Cultural Separatist Radicals
6. Marxist Structural Radicals

No one individual can be placed absolutely in one category, and positions change with time. Still, this is a useful way to approach the study of a growing body of literature that otherwise lacks focus, method, and direction.

Social scientists tend to approach popular culture from the

perspective of production. "Production" is used in its generic sense, referring to the processes of creation, manufacture, marketing, distribution, exhibiting, inculcation, evaluation, and consumption. They even refer to the "consciousness industry," which operates in the areas of art and communication, admitting that things in this "industry" change so quickly that no one, including participants and sociologists, has sufficient time to appraise the significance of the changes.[8] While they have had some success in studying "the conglomerates for the production of culture," they often seem unable to deal with the individual item, artist, or idea. No one can deny that "hard data" in the form of statistics, sales figures, polls, and graphs has been extremely important to our understanding of our culture.

The most persistent challenge leveled at "qualitative" scholarship and the humanistic approach is that it is unsystematic. Our study of culture, Claude Lévi-Strauss notes in *The Savage Mind*, is often "the pursuit of a lawless humanism." How can we evaluate codes of communication and expression if they are not in their proper context? The classic term for that context is "rhetoric," which Aristotle defined as the art of persuasion. By rejuvenating and extending that definition to all areas of communications, a new school of scholars has emerged. Their work is summarized by Thomas H. Ohlgren and Lynn M. Berk in *The New Languages: A Rhetorical Approach to the Mass Media and Popular Culture* (1977). Obviously, advertising, politics, and public propaganda address the question of rhetoric directly. They go on to analyze the "rhetoric" of film, radio television, and popular print, insisting that these are new languages with dimly perceived grammars. Each language codifies reality differently and reveals a unique metaphysics. Each offers a different perspective, a way of seeing hidden dimensions of reality.[9] What happens to a culture in which these various dimensions converge? This book attempts to answer that intriguing question.

There is a new trend to call anthologies and textbooks "rhetorical readers" that "give you models for putting your thoughts into forms that can reach and move others."[10]

Culture, rhetoric, and ice cream come in various flavors. Our goal is not so much to discover new flavors as to explain those we already have. They may have been around ever since (indeed, long before) Aristotle. I sing a song of cycles. Much of what we call "new"depends explicitly upon past models: revivals, renaissances, adaptations, and other tradition-bound forms. *Plus ça change, plus c'est la même chose.*

One lively movement at my university, for example, is the Society for Creative Anachronism. Stacy Gettier, the faculty adviser, appears at meetings in a helmet of steel, a chain mail hood, and a rivet-studded shield. "We make our own costumes, forge our own weapons and armor, collect stories about medieval times, and recreate tourneys," he says.[11] A knight by rank, Gettier admits that most members join as knights or nobles— although there is a branch made up of illiterate Vikings.

The word "illiterate" is of wide concern in the university and nation; both scholastic aptitude and written English tests have continued their annual decline. How does this relate to the lack of or need for a common culture? Will the new literacy pertain outside the printed artifact?

The man who had done much to raise that question for this generation died in the last week of 1980 at sixty-nine—Marshall McLuhan. Compelling and caustic, paradoxical and messianic, he got into the marrow of the bones of communications theory. McLuhan was a catalyst who set many of us into action and reaction. He loomed large in life, and he may grow larger in death.

The assassination of a young man that same month took on world significance. Forty-year-old John Lennon, one of the Beatles, was shot and killed in front of his New York apartment. His death hung like a pall over the holiday season and sent millions into mourning. One recalled the earlier senseless shootings of John and Robert Kennedy and of Martin Luther King, Jr. Death is always the last and the greatest of our enemies. Nothing we say or do lessens its sting. We cannot stay in strawberry fields forever.

Lennon knew that he not only shaped but also was shaped by his era. "It wasn't me, or us," he said in one of his last interviews with *Playboy* magazine. "It was the time and the place. Whatever wind was blowing at the time moved the Beatles, too. The whole boat was moving."

Perhaps the boat moves not in straight lines but in circles. The helmsmen change, not the rudder they grasp. Charting the common course is the job of Moses and Malcolm X, of Rameses and Roosevelt.

But who *knows* the common course, when the north winds blow? "Hurricane winds sweep across the American landscape," Ralph H. Gabriel noted in 1974. "What the end will be only the future can disclose."[12]

Instead of worrying about the end, let's follow the advice the king gave Alice in Wonderland and begin at the beginning . . . defining key terms and examining tradition, land and lore, myths and dreams. If, as I claimed earlier, I have something in common with Captain Ahab, let's act on his bold resolve: not to stay close to shore, where minnows dart, but to sail out into the deep—into living waters—and keep a sharp lookout for whales.

NOTES

1. Abraham Kaplan, "The Aesthetics of the Popular Arts," *Journal of Aesthetics and Art Criticism* 34 (Spring 1966), p. 351. For the antithetical viewpoint, see Dwight Macdonald, "A Theory of Mass Culture," *Diogenes* (Summer 1953).

2. See C.W.E. Bigsby, *Approaches to Popular Culture* (Bowling Green, Ohio: Popular Press, 1976) especially chapter 20.

3. For additional titles and interpretation, see John G. Cawelti, "Recent Trends in the Study of Popular Culture," *American Quarterly* (Winter 1971). His survey was updated in 1980 by Michael Marsden, in a document available from the Popular Studies Program, Bowling Green State University, Bowling Green, Ohio 43403.

4. Louis B. Wright, *Middle-Class Culture in Elizabethan England* (Chapel Hill: University of North Carolina Press, 1935), pp. 659-60. Quoted by Leo Lowenthal, *Literature, Popular Culture, and Society* (Palo Alto, Calif.: Pacific Books, 1961), p. 9.

5. Peter Laslett, *The World We Have Lost* (New York: Scribners, 1965), p. 58. See also *Family and Household in Past Time* (Cambridge: At the University Press, 1972), which Laslett edited with Richard Wall.

6. "The Discovery of Popular Culture before Printing" is Schroeder's essay in a special issue of the *Journal of Popular Culture* 11 (Winter 1977) devoted to that topic. The quotation is on p. 629. He has since edited *Five Thousand Years of Popular Culture* (Bowling Green, Ohio: Popular Press, 1980).

7. See Marshall W. Fishwick, "Do We Need Method?" in Ray Browne, Sam Grogg, and Larry Landrum, eds., *Theories and Methodologies in Popular Culture*, (Bowling Green, Ohio: Popular Press, 1978), pp. 143ff.

8. Paul DiMaggie and Paul Hirsch, "Production Organizations in the Arts," in Richard Peterson, ed., *The Production of Culture* (Beverly Hills, California: Sage Publishing, 1976), p. 83.

9. For a good introduction to the problems raised by these perspectives, see Gregory Baum, ed., *Sociology and Human Destiny* (New York: Seabury Press, 1980).

10. Paul J. Dolan and Edward Quinn. *The Sense of the Seventies: A Rhetorical Reader* (New York: Oxford, 1978), p. xvii. This book even has a separate "Rhetorical Table of Contents," classifying articles under the headings of description, exposition, argumentation, and narration.

11. For more details, see Trudy Willis, "Medieval Merriment," in Roanoke *Times and World-News*, Section C, November 3, 1980.

12. Ralph H. Gabriel. *American Values: Continuity and Change* (Westport, Conn.: Greenwood Press, 1974), p. 116.

FURTHER READING

Baum, Gregory, ed. *Sociology and Human Destiny* (New York: Seabury Press, 1980).

Enzensberger, Hans Magnus. *The Consciousness Industry* (New York: Seabury Press, 1974).

Fiedler, Leslie. *The Inadvertent Epic: From Uncle Tom's Cabin to Roots* (New York: Oxford, 1981).

Fishwick, Marshall. *Virginia: A New Look at the Old Dominion* (New York: Harpers & Row, 1959).

Furay, Conal. *The Grass-Roots Mind in America: The American Sense of Absolutes* (New York: New Viewpoints, 1977).

Gerbner, George; Gross, Larry; and Melody, William, eds. *Communications, Technology, and Social Policy* (New York: Wiley Interscience, 1973).

May, Larry. *Screening Out the Past: The Birth of Mass Culture and the Motion Picture Industry* (New York: Oxford, 1981).

Rosenblum, Ralph, and Robert, Karen. *When the Shooting Stops . . . The Cutting Begins: A Film Editor's Story* (New York: Oxford, 1980).

Wells, Alan, ed. *Mass Media and Society* (Palo Alto, Calif.: National Press Books, 1975).

2
COMMON CULTURE

''Art thou base, common and popular?''

Shakespeare, *King Henry V*

I come to praise common culture. From it flows, as from a mighty spring, all our being. Shaped by our hands and hearts and heads over countless centuries, it gives meaning to the word *human*. We can describe it as Yahweh described himself to the ancient Hebrews: ''I am what I am.''

What *are* we? Sticks and stones, schemes and dreams. Myths and legends, ideas and images. War and peace, angels and devils. We are the best that has been thought and said—we are the worst. We are, Alexander Pope noted:

> Created half to rise, and half to fall;
> Great lord of all things, yet a prey to all;
> Sole judge of truth, in endless error hurled;
> The glory, jest, and riddle of the world!

That "riddle" is older than any civilization—although each has, in turn, tried to solve it. Most civilizations of which we have any knowledge have already perished; how long ours will last is problematic. Of course, to find our roots, we have to look far behind the England from which much of our own lore and language come. There is the Judeo-Christian heritage and the Mediterranean. There is the classical world—the glory that was Greece, the grandeur that was Rome.

Rome—the very word is like a bell, booming in the time tunnel. Her imperial administration and ideas of citizenship became the basis for Western culture. Romans not only used culture (*cultus* means "to break the soil") but also exported it; there was a common culture throughout the empire. They gave this vast area a common language, common law, common purpose. Since it was for the people, they thought of it as popular (from *populus* —of or related to the general public; suitable for the majority; easy to understand). Common or popular culture grows from the earth we inhabit and cultivate.

The most remarkable thing about Roman society, and later ones that sprang from it, is that it sustained variety but insisted on cohesion. This was possible because of the media (plural of the Latin *medium*—intermediate or between). Latin was a crucial medium; so is English today, as well as all forms of print, film, radio, telephone, television, electronics. Media makes information universal and common culture possible. Seeing this, the Romans built their empire on universalism.

The master architect of this universalism, and chief transmitter of the older Greek culture, was Marcus Tullius Cicero (106-43 BC). He, more than any human being, is the hero of our story.[1] As Michael Grant points out in *The World of Rome*:

> The Renaissance was above all a Renaissance of Cicero. Even when, for purposes of communication, the national vernaculars

superseded his language, they long remained, like the morality and oratory which they expressed, beneath Cicero's spell.[2]

Bright and ambitious, he was at thirty widely regarded as the leading Roman orator. Practor at forty and consul at forty-two, Cicero made political enemies and blunders, which led to humiliating failures and compromises. Retiring to his Tusculum villa, Cicero "took refuge in writing," producing works with amazing speed—twelve major treatises and many essays in eighteen months. In addition, he was among the greatest letter writers of all times. We know Cicero better than any other Roman— indeed, better than almost any other historical figure until modern times.

But Cicero's main importance to us, in discussing common culture, is as a synthesizer and transmitter. He spent years paraphrasing, selecting, summing up—always adding his own emphasis. He adapted great works from other languages to Roman environment and taste. Marcus Tullius Cicero was one of history's greatest popularizers. With all his faults, he knew that being simple is never simple, that being widely understood is the highest achievement anyone can hope for or achieve.

For Cicero, people were central. Without their support, nothing endures. He *wanted* to promulgate a common culture, to be persuasive and enduring. The "word man" par excellence, he made Latin into a language of believable ideas and wide import, giving meaning to a massive array of earlier human thought. He made available to Rome, and all her heirs, the genius of Greece, brought over a way of thinking—the dialectical —and made possible what we now know as the academic life.

Cicero also believed in the principle of action. All parts must function in harmony with the whole, and the whole must stay in phase with nature. Hence, all creatures, all cultures have "a craving for constant activity." We should use sport, play, and merriment (as we do sleep) as means, not ends. To run, jump, and hunt is not merely to exercise the muscles but to keep the mind alert and the body *in harmony with* the mind. (Does this explain the primary role of sports and game competition over the last 2,000 years? Is it any wonder that we have today the Super

Bowl or the World Series as our chief national ritual?) We are all in this together—linked with one another, Cicero liked to say, in a single chain.

Every link is important; every effort to mend a broken chain commendable. What made Rome eternal is the chain itself. Rome left us her language, literature, laws—her art, oratory, awesome monuments. She left us the idea of both empire and ecclesia. The emperors are gone, but the popes endure. So does Rome itself: the Eternal City.

For all this—the products, insights, paradoxes—there is a single name: the Great Tradition. For centuries, this all-encompassing monomyth held Western man together, a sort of celestial glue. Then, in the seventeenth and eighteenth centuries, everything became unglued. Enormous physical and psychic changes splintered and destroyed ancient truths and superstitions: Renaissance, Reformation, Scientific Revolution, Enlightenment. The revolutionary New Learning took over the Great Tradition, leaving for everyone else what can be called the Little Tradition. What had been common culture became specialized and diverse. Instead of one, the West now had many nations, lores, theologies, traditions (elite, academic, popular, folk). Romanticism found meaning not in the community but in the individual. Existentialism denied the possibility of public or objective solutions to man's multiple problems. Everyman, who once had been the hero of epics, fables, and morality plays, was downgraded to Subman: a finite clod unmoved by a spark. He was part of the herd, the "masses" as defined by Ortega y Gasset. Blind to love and desire, Subman clung to a dull insignificant existence. His spiral pointed downward; the less he exists, the less reason there is for him to exist. Literally, nothing of the Great Tradition now moved him.

As the twenty-first century nears, a new vision has appeared. The time for reconstruction has come. Helped by a new electronic common culture and an emerging Global Village, there is hope for reviving the long-discarded Great Tradition. With pluck—and some luck with our satellites and laser beams—we may be able to put Humpty-Dumpty together again.

The material following will be exploratory, raising more

questions than it answers. The thesis set forth contains dilemmas, even contradictions: no effort will be made to conceal them. The words we deal with are encrusted with multiple meanings and nuances. I shall try to present my material as clearly as possible, hoping that the task will then be continued by others.

In common culture, thus conceived, dwell the hopes and fears of all the years. If we are to defend it, can we define it?

Of the making of definitions, there is no end. Day after day, generation after generation, the War of Words continues. Many are the casualties, few the victors. Words Fail Us. "That is not what I meant," T. S. Eliot's hapless victim says, "that is not what I meant at all." We smile, knowingly. It happens to us every day.

"Communication" itself has become a catchall, a kind of super-cliché. Now that we have a whole army of "professional" communicators, and people who teach communication, the situation takes on alarming dimensions. Richard Hoggart writes, in *Culture and Communication*:

> Our communicators combine attitudes of late-Behaviourism with a touch of the Messianic fixer, laced with elaborate jargon compounded of some applied psychology plus some neurology plus some technology.

I want to avoid Hoggart's mix, but there is no assurance that I can. We have some hope of spotting other's prejudices and shortcomings—little of seeing our own. We lack the power to see ourselves as others see us.

Let us put the toughest interpretation possible on our search and build from there. (The method would have appealed to René Descartes, who used it after arriving at *cogito, ergo sum*.) What if we neither care nor seek to communicate?

Have we moved so far from common culture that all we can construct now are air-conditioned Towers of Babel? Does the breakdown of diplomacy abroad and decency at home mean that community is eroded beyond repair?

Is anybody listening? When we claim to have "been in touch" with someone else, are we only saying that the echo chamber has worked, that we have heard the gratifying echoes of our own voices?

To understand common culture and the popular mind, we must say exactly what these words mean . . . impossible, of course, since meaning can never be exact, static, or complete. Common words in particular have multiple contradictory meanings; layers of connotations that make peeling an onion seem easy. Yet we must set some benchmarks, some boundaries.

Defining "common" takes not columns but pages in the authoritative *Oxford English Dictionary*. The very origin of the word is disputed. One possibility is the Latin *com*, meaning together, and *munis*, meaning bound or under obligation. Things are common when they are bound together, and we are obligated to share them. This is where our fellow-feeling comes from—how life becomes symbolic, significant, and shared.

Shared, joint, united; belonging to all mankind alike; possessed by the human race. "Longing the common light again to share," wrote John Dryden in 1697. Two centuries later, Robert Browning spoke of "the higher attributes of our common humanity." That light, and those attributes, are central.

I begin with the sound of John Donne's bell in my ears, tolling not just for me but for thee. We need not ask for whom the bell tolls; we already know. *Common* sense tells us, for it is part of our *common* knowledge.

Countless other concepts link up with *common*. A common carrier, such as a bus or train, is obligated to transport all who solicit the service. A common denominator works with all numbers in the equation; common law applies to all; the House of Commons, like the Book of Common Prayer, cuts through class privilege. A common right is the property of every citizen. "Do me the common right," Shakespeare has a character say in *Measure for Measure*, "to let me see them."

If defining common culture is difficult, documenting it is impossible. Since little is written down in oral cultures, and most people throughout history have been illiterate, we know next to nothing about the slave, worker or peasant in ancient Greece, imperial Rome, and medieval France—let alone in feudal Japan or tribal Africa.

There is truth in George Santayana's assertion that in the spontaneous play of his faculties man finds himself and his happiness. Or again, to quote Johan Huizanga from his classic *Homo Ludens*: "Play is an activity which proceeds within certain limits of time and space, in a visible order, outside the sphere of necessity or material utility."[3]

Sports have played a continuing major role for centuries. They were under the patronage of the Greek gods; athletes pleased not only their fans but also their deities. The word "enthusiasm" (from the Greek, *en* and *theos*) literally means "god inside." Is this not part of Shakespeare's "common right"? If the Hebrews could find God on Sinai and the Greeks on Olympus, can we be surprised that some find him today in the Super Bowl?

To be common, anything must be accepted, normative, popular. For historical and linguistic reasons, we shall emphasize common culture and refer back to it constantly.

Standing just outside, but integrally connected to the concept, is community—a social group of any shape, size, or color living together, sharing a common heritage. Such congealing is part of our nature: man, Aristotle pointed out centuries ago, is a social animal. We do not come together just to do things but to be together.

The rupture or breakdown of community sounds the death-knell of common culture and finally of humanity itself. Loneliness and alienation have been major themes in twentieth-century literature, drama, and art. The subject of Eugene Ionesco's *The Chairs*, a highly acclaimed play at mid-century, is the absence of people, the absence of the emperor, and the absence of God.

When community goes, language itself falters. Here is a passage from that same play:

"Where's my mamma? I don't have a mamma anymore."
"That's not true. I'm an orphan, hi, hi."
"My pet, my orphan, dworfan, worfan, morphan, orphan."

We are in the Zero World, where nothing can be taken for granted. We have lost community. But this is a "high culture" idea, offered by an elite (at times baffling) playwright. Common/

average/ordinary people reject the Zero World. Community is the tangible evidence of the abstract idea of common. It is the word made flesh.

A commonly used set of words helps us understand. We think of a hamlet as a small group, a village as larger, a town still larger, and a city as very large and complex. Contemporary scholars do not stop there. A metropolis can grow into a megalopolis (supercity), then into a tyrannopolis (city of tyranny), and finally into a necropolis (city of death). No matter what the political or economic plight, any inhabited place is a seat of community.

People come together to share both concepts and things: artifacts, mentifacts, icons, yearnings. They depend on language, gestures, codes, symbols. But the most important "thing" held in common escapes definition: a workable community of will, what Rousseau termed the "general will," Johann von Herder the *volksgesit*, Christian apologists the "holy spirit." Name it what you will but cling to it with all your being; this is the most precious of possessions.[4]

"All who are included in a community," wrote Saint Thomas Aquinas in his *Summa Theologica*, "stand in relation to that community as parts to the whole." Arnold Toynbee restated the idea in twentieth-century terms: "The true hallmark of the proletarian is neither poverty nor humble birth, but a consciousness of being disinherited from his ancestral place . . . being unwanted in a community which is his rightful home." Realizing this, institutions and governments strive to "create" community. They have found that it cannot be done by committee meetings, publications, or official decrees. Only when there is a deep communal dedication to ideals will community grow; indeed, then its radiance will shine forth with blinding light. True community respects the individual and his history, is immediate and real. False community centers on groups or ideologies, tends to be abstract, remote, and artificial. The end product of true community is concern, that of false community exploitation.

No one is born into a lore or community—he or she must learn about it and work at it. Communities have their own structures, codes, goals, traditions, memories. They use both a special language and a jargon. They define both orthodoxy and heresy and translate these into rules and etiquette. One defies them at great risk.

Organic community (gemeinschaft) and atomistic community (gesellschaft) have their own lores. The organic is small and cozy—a band of brothers. The atomistic is large and impersonal —office workers or factory employees. Organic community shrinks as the need for the atomistic grows. We leave the small tranquil town to live in the large bustling city. We join the lonely crowd. But is this interpretation too simplistic? If (as Daniel Bell suggests) we substitute "total" for organic and "individual" for atomistic, the situation changes. There is much tyranny in small towns—much real individual freedom in big cities. Are not the chances for innovation, creativity, and growth much enhanced by separation from the womb? From the community?

Can there be a merging, a blending? Can community be built on organic individualism? Can the individual relate to multitudes of specialties and become "himself"? If we are willing to accept things as they are, can we share both gemeinschaft and gesellschaft?

American Studies, a field launched after World War II, has asked these questions scores of times, without clear answers. The earliest notion of the field was basically geographical and political; it was an "area study." In the 1950s, the emphasis was on a *holistic* alternative and on the axiom that "a civilization as a whole is greater than the sum of its parts." The culture concept became central, stressing the functional wholeness of the national culture through customs, behavior, institutions, and values. Here, many thought, was a suitable framework for whatever we might want to study—including popular culture. Then a new group of literary and cultural historians, known as the Myth/Image/Symbol School, took over leadership. They chronicled myths of American origins and character built on specific ideas and events. Myths, images, and symbols are progressively more complex stages of the same thing and embody an all-encompassing conception of reality.[5] Since 1970, a "third generation" of American Studies has attempted to replace the Myth/

Image/Symbol School with work built on anthropology, disguised under the name of American Ethnophysics. They have not had much effect on popular culture. The simple fact is that *no* satisfactory methodology has been worked out in the last generation.[6] As soon as one group thinks it understands things as they are, another one comes along to challenge and replace it. We stand on not-so-common ground.

Despite new insights and powerful critiques, the Marxist framework has proven to be restrictive. There is a wide range of Marxist work, not to be dismissed without careful examination; work by American, English, and French critics has greater flexibility than that of most Russians and Eastern Europeans and involves correlations between Marxism and many other philosophical and social scientific perspectives. No longer concerned exclusively with sociology and philosophy, Marxism has spilled over into literary criticism, aesthetics, education, theology, anthropology, and popular culture. Terry Eagleton, Max Horkheimer, Theodor Adorno, Walter Benjamin, and Herbert Marcuse have led the way.[7]

A basic premise with this school of thought is that the production of ideas, concepts, and consciousness is first of all directly interwoven with the language of real life. Consciousness does not determine life: life determines consciousness. Art and literature are not mysteriously inspired; they are forms of perception, ways of seeing. They relate to the social mentality or ideology of an age. That ideology, in turn, is the product of the concrete social relations into which we enter at a particular time and place . . . to what we called "grass roots" in our introduction.[8]

Well aware of the power of media to convey such notions, Marxist critics have made good use of film and television. The brilliant young English critic, John Berger, made a widely acclaimed series of Marxist films in 1972 called *Ways of Seeing*. By examining a set of relations between artist and audience (producer/consumer/vendor/purchaser), he reveals both fine and popular arts as types of property relations. Thus, he gives us a new premise on which to explore contemporary culture.

But the basic premise that hobbles Marxism is stated by

Grigori Oganov in the "official" publication *Genuine Culture and False Substitutes*:

> All forms of literature and art influence people. At one time they were a mystic power; poets were equated with priests. Rejecting all mysticism, realism has increased this power tenfold; socialist realism has given this power the strength of class analysis and social forethought.[9]

Some idea of the level of dogmatism that is employed can be had from this passage:

> All the wheels of big business and advertising are turning day and night to prove the colossal lie that America is smiling [p. 65].

Unexpected events or factors negate such formulas. Take, for example, the American Baby Boom, which was occurring even as dramatists like Ionesco were imagining a Doom Boom. From 1946 to 1953, the number of babies born in the United States rose about 50 percent. This is by far the greatest increase in births ever recorded here or (until then) in any other country. This plummeted the center of population gravity from age thirty-five in 1958 to age seventeen in 1963. How would community, culture, life-style be altered?

The number of babies born, and the increase in young adults, can be tabulated and recorded—facts. But what they *mean*, and how internal changes make up other forms of hidden truth—is taken on faith. No one can measure or cultivate faith or say where faith comes from. It involves primitive longings, promises, fulfillments. Faith is central to the simple operation of society. Had I not believed the barker who promised me a look at the whale, I would not have dropped my dime into the bucket. Had I not believed we can analyze and understand basic aspects of popular culture, I would not have written this book. The central core of faith is metaphysics. This is what moves mountains.

For the body of faith, we have a special word—tradition. Those who embody it are traditional. To that word, and those people, we now turn.

NOTES

1. From the whole library by and about Cicero, two recent books of merit are Elizabeth Rawson's *Cicero, A Portrait* (London: Allen Lane, 1975), and W. K. Lacey's *Cicero and the End of the Roman Republic* (New York: Barnes and Noble, 1978). As for his own work, there are six volumes in the Penguin Classics paperback series, with splendid introductions by leading scholars.

2. Michael Grant, *The World of Rome* (New York: Mentor Books, 1960), p. 320.

3. Johan Huizanga, *Homo Ludens* (Boston: Beacon Press, 1950), p. 233.

4. See Simone Weil, *The Need for Roots* (New York: Bantam, 1954).

5. See Rene Welleck and Austin Warren, *Theory of Literature*, (New York: Harcourt Brace, 1963), especially chapter 15.

6. Jay Mechling, "In Search of American Ethnophysics," in Luther S. Luedtke, *The Study of American Culture: Contemporary Conflicts* (Deland, Fla.: Everett Edwards, 1977), chapter 10.

7. Matthew L. Lamb, "The Challenge of Critical Theory," in Gregory Baum, ed., *Sociology and Human Destiny* (New York: Seabury Press, 1980). In addition to an analysis of new theories, the chapter contains a long helpful bibliography.

8. For a full development of this position, see Terry Eagleton, *Marxism and Literary Criticism* (London: Methuen, 1976). Eagleton discusses John Berger's films in chapter 4, "The Author as Producer." Marxist criticism, Eagleton concludes, "is part of our liberation from oppression, and that is why it is worth discussing at book length."

9. Grigori Oganov, *Genuine Culture and False Substitutes* (Moscow: Novoisti Press, 1979), p. 9.

FURTHER READING

Bigsby, C.W.E., ed. *Approaches to Popular Culture* (Bowling Green: University Popular Press, 1976).

Cannel, Ward, and Macklin, June. *The Human Nature Industry* (New York: Doubleday, Anchor Press, 1973).

Hoggart, Richard. *On Culture and Communication* (New York: Oxford, 1972).

Longergan, Bernard. *Insight: A Study of Human Understanding* (New York: Harper & Row, 1978).

Rosenberg, Bernard, and White, David Manning. *Mass Culture: The Popular Arts in America* (London: Collier-Macmillan, 1957).

Schramm, Wilbur. *Men, Messages, and Media: A Look at Human Communication* (New York: Harper & Row, 1973).

Williams, Raymond. *Culture and Society, 1780-1950* (London: Chatto & Windus, 1960).

_____. *The Long Revolution* (New York: Columbia University Press, 1961).

3

THE GREAT TRADITION

"Should you ask me, when these stories?
Whence these legends and traditions?"

Henry Longfellow, *The Song of Hiawatha*

Culture is the child of continuity. Those things that we lead
across or hand down make up our tradition (two Latin words,
trans, meaning across, and *ducio*, to lead or hand down).

By word and deed, tradition is an expression of the general
will—the distilled essence of what people cherish and think
worth retaining. All surviving societies are traditional, no matter
how fast the rate of change. Jews use the concept to describe a
body of laws and doctrines received from Moses and handed

down orally from generation to generation. Christians see tradition as a body of essential teachings delivered by Christ and His apostles. So it has been with other religions and races everywhere. To have no tradition is to have no past, that is, to be nobody.

Put differently, tradition sets the parameters of our past; culture provides the framework in which we operate. Things shared in common define our humanity. To governments, tradition gives prestige; to communities, pride; to writers, themes; to artists, symbols. Drawing from both fact and fiction, tradition is superhistorical—slow to form and even slower to die.

Tradition may be misused and distorted, perverted to despicable ends. It can help to preserve ignorance and bigotry, justify crimes, thwart men of goodwill, destroy the very culture from which it rose. These traditions wither and die. Those that endure and grow stronger are as close as mankind ever gets to enduring truth.

Tradition is easily observed in a tribal society—isolated, intimate, self-sufficient. Audience participation is important, tasks are shared, riddles are answered in chorus. In such a society (the Tiv of Nigeria, for example), if a carver is called away from his work, another tribesman may pick up the knife and continue the carving. Organic wholeness is part of the Great Tradition.

All this changes as societies become complex. Anthropologist Robert Redfield, in *Peasant Society and Culture*, suggested a model that has been widely adopted. There are, he said, two cultural streams in most societies—the Great Tradition of the educated minority and the Little Tradition of all the rest:

> The Great Tradition is cultivated in schools and temples. The Little Tradition works itself out and keeps going in the lives of the unlettered in their small communities. The two traditions are interdependent.

In this book, I shall apply that model to contemporary America, extending or modifying as necessary. I shall also draw from those who have applied it elsewhere—such as Peter Laslett in England and Peter Burke in Europe. In *Popular Culture in Early*

Modern Europe, Burke uses Redfield's model with great insight and success. He notes that what Redfield calls "the Great Tradition" included the classical heritage, medieval theology, the Renaissance, Scientific Revolution, and Enlightenment. Left to the Little Tradition — and the peasants, yeomen, and paupers — were folklore, devotional images, mystery places, farces, festivals, and broadsides. Well into "modern times" (the sixteenth and seventeenth centuries) both traditions had a common source. So great was its power that this source sustained the Age of Discovery. Swashbucklers and settlers from Spain, Portugal, Holland, France, and Britain set sail in small wooden boats for distant lands. Common culture girdled the globe in the seventeenth century—as it would do again, in an entirely different way, in the twentieth.

America was settled in that earlier outburst. Hardy bands from old England settled in New England and along the east coast of North America. Mainly from rural areas and the lower classes, they were saturated with an essentially medieval common culture, which enabled them to found a new nation in the "howling wilderness."

Community was the key, ingenuity the weapon. Aristocrats and elitists who came over had to "root hog or die." A good example, William Byrd, hacked out a plantation on the James River, laid out the town of Richmond, and surveyed the disputed Virginia-North Carolina border. As his *Secret Diary* makes clear, it was no picnic. Indians stole his food. The Dismal Swamp was dismal. Byrd's aristocratic companions behaved in most ungentlemanly fashion. Cornering a country bumpkin, "they examined all her hidden Charms and played a great many gay Pranks." When things got too bad, the chaplain "rubbed up" these proto-Rover Boys with a "seasonable sermon."

Even sermons did not always help. One of the commissioners, whom Byrd nicknamed Firebranch, became so annoyed with a fellow that he picked up a table leg "big enough to knock down whom Byrd nicknamed Firebrand, became so annoyed with a Firebrand was saluted with a long line of titles, the most acceptable of which was "son of a whore." So it went.

Later, Byrd returned to the forests to survey 20,000 acres of

Roanoke River bottomland—there to confront again and describe the lubbers, thickskulls, and common buckskins. Anyone who believes in the Noble Savage should read Byrd's description of the common folk who were struggling on the frontier. The males, he recorded, "lye abed and Snore, till the Sun has run one third of his course. Having arisen and lit their pipes, they venture out under the protection of a cloud of smoke. Thus they loiter away their lives, like Solomon's Sluggard, with their arms across, and at the winding up of the year scarcely have bread to it."

What of the women? Byrd describes one with unkempt hair, part of which she brought decently forward. "The rest dangled behind quite down to the rump, like one of Herodotus' East Indian pigmies."

Although William Byrd had the best library in the colonies—over 3,600 volumes—most Americans depended on the oral culture that had sustained mankind since time immemorial. "I thank God we have not free schools nor printing," wrote Virginia Governor William Berkeley in 1671, "and I hope we shall not have these hundred years." Later, when the rebellious George Washington had to write to his generals, he used odd scraps of paper—there was nothing better to be had. But there *was* a common culture. Folktales and legends that had flourished for centuries in Europe (about monsters, mermaids, ghosts, St. Elmo's fire, whales) traveled to the New World, as chroniclers like John Winthrop, Thomas Morton, William Wood, and Increase and Cotton Mather prove. Cotton Mather advised ministers (in *Manuductio*) to have "an Inexhaustible Store of Stories" for the pulpit; doubtless, many of them did. The devil and witches abounded. Some people were actually executed in New England's great witchcraft delusion.

There was much material about the Indian. Assumed to be in league with the devil, Indians were the heavies in captivity stories, which Russel B. Nye calls (in *The Unembarrassed Muse*) "the first authentically popular American novels." The best was by Mary Rowlandson. She was captured by Indians in 1675, "enslaved to atheistical, proud, wild, cruel, barbarous, brutish [in one word] diabolical creatures." Her graphic opening still strikes terror in the reader's heart. A suckling child was "knockt in the head.'' When a man pleaded with them for mercy, they ''knockt him in head, and stript him naked, and split open his Bowels.''

In such lives, we see how old memories and new environment melded into a great and complex community. This is the soil out of which tradition, meaning, and stability grew.

By the time of the French and American revolutions, in the late eighteenth century, a momentous schism was occurring on both sides of the Atlantic. The wealthy and well-educated, Burke demonstrates, had begun to develop a distinct and separate ''way of life'' with different presuppositions and styles. This powerful elite abandoned common culture to the lower classes. They separated themselves, withdrew from old ways, set themselves apart by dress, manner, and even language. This withdrawal did not take place in any one generation, but occurred at different times and places. Eventually, the gap between elite and common culture widened. Oral and visual traditions could not absorb rapid change, while academic ''book culture'' changed with unprecedented speed. A great twentieth-century poet, William Butler Yeats, reduced this abstraction to a concrete poetic metaphor. He has John Locke (hard-headed philosopher of the new day) falling into a swoon, after which God takes the spinning jenny from his side. That instrument and the ensuing Industrial Revolution will smash the old traditions and beliefs into innumerable small pieces.

Others put the credit (or the blame) on other shoulders. Many feel that the chief instigator was René Descartes, whose *Essay on Method* prepared the way for a scientific world with its own Great Tradition. This would be based on ruthless, rational thinking and on the language of mathematics. Myth, superstition, poetry, and mystery would be ruled out—that would be left to the Little Tradition.

The New Science proposed a creed that began: ''I believe in one God, the mathematical, not interested in being almighty, but concerned instead with logical equations.'' Following this, the physical sciences achieved new prestige and power. A whole cluster of ''social'' sciences sprang up. The humanities, long the center of learning, lost their supremacy. People turned from painting to photography, from philosophy to psychology. Literature retreated into formal meters, flowers into formal gardens. And scientists both operated and explained things.

Craftsmen, woodsmen, and peasants continued their old ways, as the chief carriers of common/popular culture. What were those ways, those beliefs? Unless we know them, we cannot understand the Great Schism that took place.

Traditional Man inherited centuries of wisdom, experience, and learning: he was radically related to reality. Believing in the dust-to-dust cycle and in mysteries he was not meant to fathom, Traditional Man saw purpose woven into every aspect of daily life. The repetition of stories, seasons, and events had great meaning. When it was dry, he prayed to God for rain. When his child was sick, he asked the Blessed Virgin to intercede. Like the animals he raised and slaughtered and the crops he harvested, he was bound to the earth.

He knew stories of the saints, kings, and martyrs and believed them implicitly. He also believed in fairy tales, which were stories of enchantment—a blending of the obvious and the impossible. In them, poetic justice triumphed and the unrecognized were made known. No fairy-tale teller or believer can be a relativist. To survive is to believe absolutely.

Our archetypal figure enjoyed carnivals and roared at the antics of clowns and charlatans. Year after year, he saw characters and skits that were already familiar to him. The plights of Patient Griselda, the Ugly Duckling, or Saint George were as real to him as were the people in his family or village. They were timeless because they were part of a transcendent reality. The God who had time to watch every sparrow fall never let the human race get out of hand. All the deserving lived happily ever after. Heartened by this thought, plagues, pests, and mothers-in-law could be endured.

Although his cosmology was prescientific, Traditional Man was both sensitive and sensible. For him, words were symbolic. He knew that booklore turns pale beside folklore, that to be loved leaders must be heroic, and that enduring memories are mythic. He did not believe that only alchemists dwelt in the realms of gold. Common sense and uncommon learning were all of one piece. Millions of people, living and dying over hundreds of years, were Traditional.

Authority on earth was centered in a continuously inspired church. For the Western world, all roads led to Rome, all thoughts to God. Sacraments were the means to grace. Christendom was another name for community. Life on earth, this City of Satan, was nasty, brutish, and short. But the deserving could look forward to eternal bliss in the City of God.

Traditional Man drew substance from nature, not media; he worked with men, not machines. He was rooted in and regulated by the seasons. He knew what he knew.

There was a healthy tension, not a gulf, between mind and feeling, percept and concept. Reason and revelation were allies, not antagonists. Although formal learning was extremely limited, a vigorous folk culture flourished. So did folklore, the outcropping of the poetic nature of man and of his innate sense of wonder. Folklore is connected with the mystery and wonder of the earth, which most Traditional Men tilled daily. Folk wisdom and creativity emerged in songs, dramas, dances, legends, and tales. People in a folk culture entertain themselves; those in a mass culture are entertained. When folklore passes from a people, much that is glorious and splendid vanishes.

Today, the very word "folklore" implies for some a condescension toward backward people—Australian Bushmen, Siberian Eskimos, Southern Negroes. Folklore is equated with naive belief, while those things we sophisticated moderns believe deserve the label "truth."

Such a decline is only one of many consequences of the changeover. Nationalism, secularism, urbanism, capitalism, and science are among the causal factors. Men tired of archaic archangels, but not of religion.

Many voices tell of the birth of the Modern World. Secularization of the West came in stages. The process was under way by the end of the eleventh century, when Pope Gregory VII insisted that the king was a layman, with no special sacramental power. A century later, Thomas of Aquinas held that reason was not specifically Christian but "natural." In effect, he enthroned reason in the secular world and destroyed the position of men like Anselm who saw reason as the way of mediating on faith.

The new secularism came from many sources, many voices. This was a central notion: let man take over. Let the world be the world for the world's sake—and as an ultimate value. The extraordinary success of the New Learning and New Science created a new elite. They (not the common people) became the bearers of the Great Tradition. Those who did not understand or endorse it were split off, left behind. Theirs was the traditional, the Little when measured against the Great. Common culture was split, and class struggle was inevitable. From the viewpoint of popular culture, this was the Great Schism.

Not everyone agrees that it ever occurred. Alan Gowans thinks that art's four main functions continued unabated, with only surface changes in nomenclature and social preference. Art is always concerned with substitute imagery, illustration, conviction and persuasion, and beautification. Gowans elaborates:

> In Western culture up to about 1750, the activity that was called art always involved performing at least one of these functions, and what was called Great Art frequently involved them all. What is called Art today has come to perform none of these functions, except incidentally.

What happened to the functions art *used* to perform? They were assumed by "popular" artists: photographers, illustrators, designers, and cartoonists. Essentially, Gowans and I perceive the same result, although we analyze it differently.

Because Burke and others have documented the split and because the resulting class consciousness, socioeconomic barriers, and educational levels have been powerful forces for generations, I shall not detail these matters here. (Numerous sociology and history books do the job.) Instead, I will explore the reuniting of the cultures since 1945. The gap that was so gradually opened is being dramatically closed. Called "popular" culture, the Little Tradition, or common culture, has picked up new power and meaning. Radical change has affected the lower and middle classes more than the upper. Radio, television, and circuitry have torn down the old barriers, heralding the Age of Electronic Equality.

The *second* Industrial Revolution has reversed the trends and meaning of the first, has changed the emphasis from the Great to the Little Tradition, and has created a new international style that is only dimly understood. No one was more responsible for these remarkable changes than Thomas A. Edison. By inventing (or at least marketing) the electric light bulb, motion-picture machine, and phonograph, he opened up mass communications. Indeed, he did something more startling—he invented "inventing" as we know it today. His strategy was to establish the need for a new product, raise money for the necessary research, do it, plan the merchandising, and put the profits back to foster new inventions. A generation later, fields like advertising, media studies, product planning, and public relations flourished.

Another godfather—some say the chief one—was Henry Ford. Raised in rural Michigan, where common culture still held sway, he hated farming and went to Detroit. There, Ford took a job at the Edison Company, rising from night fireman to chief engineer. In 1903, he set up the Ford Motor Company; in 1908, he produced his first Model T; in 1913, he built his first assembly line. In so doing, he put America on wheels and changed our common culture.[2]

Throughout his life, Ford was suspicious of social innovation, even though he was responsible for much of it. Black cats, broken mirrors, and coincidences terrified him. Yet by combining Eli Whitney's system of interchangeable parts and Oliver Evan's system of mechanical conveyors, he added new elements to common culture that would infiltrate every area of the globe. His life stretched from Gettysburg to Hiroshima—from horses to atom bombs—and he smacked of the legendary. He was a mechanical Peter Pan who never grew up, the sorcerer's apprentice who could make the broom carry water yet could not make it stop and a Frankenstein who could invent a robot that conquered its maker. He might even be seen as a Prometheus who stole the secret of mechanized living from heaven.

A generation of technocrats led by Edison and Ford make the old common culture an integral part of the new technology. They did it by offering the Magnificent Bribe: everyone can enjoy every scientific advance and every material advantage— *provided* he takes everything offered, in the precise style and quantity the system requires. Electronic culture leads to enforced obsolescence. The motto is "Waste not, have not." The inherent danger of this obsolescence is stressed by Roger Burlingame in *Backgrounds of Power*:

> If we continue to place God in the machine, we shall be at the mercy not of the machine, but of its high priests who know better and are thus in a position to exploit our ignorance.

If the danger was great, so was the achievement. As the culture changed, so did the tradition. A combination of technology, ideology, and mobility DID reinstate common culture.

The merging of mechanical and electrical power has produced such spectacular new weapons and systems (missiles, satellites, robots, space fantasies) that we seldom think of it as reviving old forms and lores. Yet that is exactly what has happened. The new stress on ear-learning has awakened aspects of the preprint culture. Tribal rituals have returned—meeting in front of the television set is an obvious example. The term "retribalization" has even been used to describe the phenomenon. We shall give it another name: the return of common culture.

Groups that have long been "outside the community" are being taken back in. The subservient sex is demanding a new and unqualified equality. (Who would have thought, a generation ago, that registration for the draft might include females as well as males? Yet that had been advocated by former President Carter in 1980.) Once more, there are no more "invisible men," a term often applied to black Americans. Assumed, then forced, to be inferior, Afro-Americans shuffled, bowed, and played the buffoon.[3] The stereotypes persisted well into the twentieth century, as black writer Langston Hughes showed. He invented Simple, a fictional stereotype of World War II blacks, who made cranks in a defense factory. "You've been working there for months," Simple's girlfriend said. "By now you oughta know what them cranks crank."

"Aw woman," Simple replied, "you know white folks don' tell black folks what cranks crank!" And vice versa. The lack of genuine racial understanding and interchange has been a major tragedy of American history. Of all the avenues that have opened, none has been more productive than popular culture. The 1960s were, in terms of racial tension, our baptism by fire. Insights were shared, adjustments made. When the bicentennial came, much remained to be done. But at the 1976 Democratic National Convention, black Georgia Congressman Andrew Young could tell the nation that he was "laying down the burden of race" and could urge black Americans to vote for a southern politician (Jimmy Carter) whose father had been a militant racist only a generation earlier.

It was not strange that the Martin Luther Kings and the Andrew Youngs came from the Deep South; from the rural South and urban North (the plantation and the ghetto), much black popular culture springs. The intertwining and interacting of African, Latin, and Anglo-Saxon elements in Dixie produced a unique synthesis—jazz, for example. Unlike Washington Irving and Herman Melville, black and white Southerners did not have to flee to Spain or Tahiti to find fresh material; they only had to look outside their window.

Dixie's Black Belt (as W. J. Cash points out in *The Mind of the South*) had many grave weaknesses, such as a narrow concept of social responsibility, attachment to fictions and false values, sentimentality, lack of realism. But it also had the ability to see tragic dimensions. Not Massachusetts but Mississippi produced William Faulkner and Walker Percy.

Contemporary black writers have tried to define and isolate unique ingredients and qualities of black America. Al Hollingsworth wants his paintings to be "as far from the mainstream of recent art as Aretha Franklin is from Frank Sinatra." Black artist Danny Johnson seeks to "transcend his blackness," adding, "I don't want to be tied down in a racial category."[4] Being black in America is suddenly a strength and advantage, after decades of being a barrier and handicap; an intense force that has infiltrated the entire culture; an international force that goes far beyond our boundaries:[5] one only has to listen to white teenagers to know how powerful the impact of blacks has been. For a time, black separatism flourished; there were efforts to create a "black Christmas mythology," with black snow and a song called "I'm Dreaming of a Black Christmas." One of the largest toy companies, Shinadana, marketed a black talking doll that said "Cool it, Baby" and "Can you dig it?"

To "dig it"—to produce a portrait of a collective identity—is not easy. To know what blacks have contributed since they arrived in the New World, we must study their popular culture. Much was neither preservable nor preserved—mainly oral, not written; casual, not formal; clandestine, not overt. We must look not only to archives and written records but also to every available source.

One major, and largely untapped, resource is photograph and film archives. There we can discover not only physical but psychological truths and clues. As Seigfried Kracauer points out in *Theory of Film: The Redemption of Physical Reality*, moviemakers and audiences engage in muted dialogues on form and formula. Films are, among many other things, mechanisms of social integration, transmitters of popular ideas, confirmers of stereotypes. We believe what appears on the screen because it confirms what we believe.

The great physical and historical reality for black Americans is chattel slavery. Not until the Civil War ended in 1865 did the 4 million slaves join the 400,000 free Negroes and the 27 million non-Afro-Americans in enjoying the benefits of liberty; the rapid imposition of segregation and Jim Crow laws often rescinded it. Much of the behavior of Americans (white and black, North and South, young and old) is understandable only against this background.

"Uncle Tom," one of the major black stereotypes, comes out of this history. Harriet Beecher Stowe's *Uncle Tom's Cabin* (1852) had an enormous impact around the world. When she went abroad, the reception given to the American author of the famous attack on slavery was little short of hysterical. She had become symbolic.

So had Uncle Tom, the long-suffering, subservient slave who loved even those who hated and abused him. Ever since, "Tom" has symbolized one who chooses not to fight back, to remain faithful even to those who destroy him. The infant movie industry produced a twelve-minute *Uncle Tom's Cabin* as early as

1903. In it, Tom (played by a famous black minstrel star, Sam Lucas) died in the arms of his white master. In the second motion-picture version (1913), Tom was played by a white actor, Harry Pollard; a black actor, James Lowe, played the 1926 title role in a way acceptable to the white audience.

Artistic performance can never be divorced from political reality. During the years of the early films, Jim Crow laws were spreading throughout America, and the temporary gains made during the Reconstruction period were being wiped out. Historians point out that twenty-two blacks from the South served with distinction in Congress between 1870 and 1901. The last of these, Representative George H. White of North Carolina, said, "We are forging head, slowly perhaps." The analysis of Booker T. Washington, given in an 1895 Atlanta speech, was more accurate: "It is at the bottom of life we must begin, and not at the top."

Sixty years later, major civil rights legislation was enacted by Congress; a generation after that, the plight of minorities had made giant leaps forward. Old "traditions" had crumbled, new mores were sanctioned. The part that mass media (especially television) had in all this is immeasurable. So was the impact of change here at home on the rest of the world—two-thirds of which is nonwhite.

Traditions grow and, if they survive, change. What were recently seen as parts of a "new electric culture" have themselves become traditional, the norm; the well-established items, in size, shape, and design, part of our way of life, part of the American *tradition.*

Hence, they have attained status and sanctity. They have their loyal following, their staunch supporters. We expect the electric toaster to perform every morning and to prepare our toast "just right." We are disoriented by any other way, any other sound than that pop-up that (along with the chug-a-chug of the electric percolator) identifies breakfast, launch-off, and "the way things start at our house." Those who affect us most are not necessarily those we see and hear in the flesh. Let me give an example.

I did not meet him until the youth of my old age—and the only place I ever saw him was on television. His name was Jacob

Bronowski, and he talked about *The Ascent of Man.* After a few weeks of watching his wonderful hands and listening to his wise words, I learned that he had died suddenly, just after finishing the series. How typically twentieth century: to make friends with an already-dead man—electronically.

And how wonderful. Images and actions beyond the grave. Electronic immortality. An audio-visual epistle, *simultaneously* available to the Romans, Corinthians, New Yorkers, and Podunk Cornerites.[6]

The program that impressed me most was "The Long Childhood." Our civilization, Bronowski points out, adores above all else the symbol of the child. For most of history, children were made to conform to the image of the adult. What I have seen, in my life time, is a dramatic reversal: adults conforming to the image of their children. Tradition has been upended.

The children: the Beatles, Elvis, Bob Dylan, Otis Redding, Joan Baez, John Denver, Elton John. . . . What magnificent teachers![7] They are part of the new common culture, as well as the Great Tradition. They help provide the continuity that will allow us to survive and flourish in years to come.

NOTES

1. Alan Gowans, *The Unchanging Arts* (Philadelphia: Lippincott, 1971), p. 13.

2. The most comprehensive biography is Allan Nevin's *Ford: The Times, the Man, the Company* (New York: Scribners, 1954). See also Keith Sward, *Legend of Henry Ford* (New York: Russell, 1948).

3. This is documented by Lemuel A. Johnson, *The Devil, the Gargoyle, and the Buffoon: The Negro as Metaphor in Western Literature* (New York: Dutton, 1971).

4. See Marshall W. Fishwick, *Contemporary Black Artists* (New York: Sandak, 1966), chapter 2.

5. See Addison Gale, Jr., *Towards a Black Aesthetic* (New York: Weybright and Talley, 1971), and Armstead Robinson, ed., *Black Studies in the University* (New Haven: Yale University Press, 1969).

6. Some of this new potential is explored by R. J. Janaro and T. C. Altshuler in *The Art of Being Human: The Humanities as a Technique for Living* (New York: Scribners, 1979).

7. Jac L. Tharpe's *Elvis: Images and Fancies* (New York: Basic Books, 1980) attempts to show how youth, charisma, and popularity have come together in such extraordinary careers as that of Elvis Presley, who died in 1978.

FURTHER READING

Burner, David; Marcus, Robert D.; and Tilson, Cori, eds. *America Through the Looking Glass: A Historical Reader in Popular Culture* (Englewood Cliffs, N.J.: Prentice-Hall, 1974).

DeMott, Benjamin. *Supergrow: Essays and Reports on Imagination in America* (New York: E. P. Dutton, 1969).

Eliot, T. S. *Tradition and the Individual Talent* (New York: Harcourt Brace, 1936).

Gilbert, Felix. *The End of the European Era, 1890 to the Present* (New York: W. W. Norton, 1979).

Haskell, Molly. From *Reverence to Rape: The Treatment of Women in the Movies* (New York: Penguin, 1980).

4
LAND AND LORE

"Ye shall eat the fat of the land."

Book of Genesis

Ashes to ashes, dust to dust. We share a common culture, a common dirt. With that dirt, and land, come the power and the glory. The land is the *mysterious tremendous* (tremendous mystery), and its yearly renewal is the supreme miracle. Our daily bread is our holy communion.[1]

Traditional Man knew and believed this over the centuries. The sacred and profane blended, and each day was an epiphany. In the new Electric Age, when milk comes from bottles and food from cans, will the *mysterious tremendous* survive?

The answer may rest with our land and lore.

Look at the map of your state or region. Can we translate those lines and names into community? Do flat maps point to actual three-dimensional existence? Do maps show people, games, harvests? Of course not. Yet all buildings, games, and food come from that land. Womb of life, the earth is our Alpha and our Omega—our beginning and our end. Common culture is earthbound.

Men and soil interact in countless subtle ways. The landscape and its use mirror the myriad paths people tread, generation after generation, in the unending search for meaning and self-expression. Man plus nature give history's basic equation. The relationship is mutual, primordial, and essential. The influence of nature (direct and indirect) is the major force in our lives.

Individuals write with pencils; culture marks with plows and trowels. The basic human story is written on the face of the land. The appearance of pastures, gullies, furrows; city blocks, log cabins, slums, junk heaps—pieced together and interpreted, furnish a commentary more profound than all the histories ever written.

"Landscape" means many things. On a hillside, the poet sees intimations of immortality; the engineer, a new sewer line. A farmer translates an acre of land into so many bushels of wheat; a soldier into so many places for cannon; an oil driller into so many potential drill sites; the architect as a place for a gas station. The same land can be used dozens of ways, depending on the user. We see what we are prepared to see—the mind trains the eye. Seldom do two people, living together, perceive the same things. Landscape is the state of being of a place, derived from the inhabitant's inner mind. Landscape is for the historian what gestalt is for the psychologist—a totality of aspect.

The "sense of space" (another term for landscape perception) varies greatly. Primitive people are literally limited to the horizon. The Ancient World eventually encompassed the inner sea, the Mediterranean. From this vast basin came much of the common culture for Western civilization. How did our ancient forebears, clustered near the coastline in what came to be called Africa, western Asia, and southern Europe, view the land that sustained them?

They thought of it as sacred and worshipped both land and water in epic, myth, and song. Although preoccupied with the environment (as the ancient arts in Egypt, Persia, Turkey, and Greece illustrate), they had few schemes for altering it. Nature had purpose and design (*telos* in Greek). Humans accepted this or defied it at their own peril. Only centuries later, when the Age of Science began, would nature become (at least for the common man) the framework of rationally contrived structure, the stage for human progress. At this very moment, nature would be desacralized: what a huge price we paid for our gadgets and comforts!

The earliest metaphor for unexploited nature was the garden. The people whose land and imaginations brought forth the three major religions that still most shape our culture—Jewish, Christian, and Moslem—started their Old Testament with the Garden of Eden. In the 1980s, when that garden has become a battleground once again, we recall our paradise lost.

For millions of immigrants, paradise was regained (in myth, if not in reality) by coming to the Brave New World. So try to imagine how to the first explorers "earth's only paradise" must have looked in the mind's eye, and frequently in the body's eye: vast and varied, unmeasured and unfenced, dotted with sassafras and sumac, with wild strawberry and hart's tongue. The virgin woods were "full of pease, pumpions, and chinquapins." The air was soft as pinfeathers. Succulent birds and beasts had never heard the hunter's horn. This was the Brave New World; these were the immigrants who would conquer it.[2]

"Conquer" is a big word, for this land was (as the Indians said) "strong medicine." Europeans wanted to know: "What will we do to the land?" They seldom asked: "What will the land do to us?"

Landscape and culture are Siamese twins. Men leave their bounties, bodies, and history in the earth, which is the womb and hub of life. This alone can they seize and shape; only from this can they come and go.

The Indian's approach to America is basically religious; the white man's, economic. This irreconcilable difference estranged the two races and all but deprived the Indian of his right to exist on his prehistoric homeland. It also cost the white man his opportunity to make peace with the earth, for there has long been something demonic in his relentless exploitation of it.

Although poor in legal tender, Indians have been rich in ceremony and understanding. Their bold colors and primordial gestures mirror the spiritual drama of life in America. Their wisdom and experience have been distilled in the hunt and the sacrifice. "They had what the world has lost," writes John Collier in *Indians of the Americas.* "They have it now. What the world has lost, the world must have again, lest it die. Not many years are left to have or not have, to recapture the lost ingredient." To find that ingredient has become a major quest of our time.

The Indians' grain (corn or maize) was central, as were wheat for Europeans and rice for Asians. Unlike many crops, corn cannot reproduce itself; there is no such thing as a "wild" ear of corn. When a man dies, the cornfield perishes with him. But the corn lived, sustaining an ever-increasing red as well as white population.

White men adapted Indian methods and crops to survive. European broadcast seeding failed in many areas, and the Indians' hill-planting method was adopted. One central lesson all newcomers had to learn: the American earth is a power to be reckoned with and feared.

Take our sun, which has scorched a hole in American culture. Beside it, the English sun looks like a faded shilling. Or consider the ugly hurricanes that masquerade behind names like Allen, Doris, or Evelyn. America is plagued by the continental waywardness of rampaging nature, by violence and paradox, by the cold blue wind in the day and the hot human blues in the night. Here nature can rumble, roar, gurgle, and be majestically silent. Only Robert Redford's cunning, Road-Runner's cussedness, and Wonder Woman's power can cope with it. West of the Mississippi is a wild, bone-breaking landscape, fit for uncouth exiled gods.

In the East, civilization rests on water, timber, and land. In the Great Plains, the first two props are missing. Inventions ranging from barbed wire and six-shooters to combines and cotton sleds have made it possible for men to live there: live, not conquer.

From the beginning, America's story has been one of painful separation and slow adjustment—the saga of caravans venturing out from citadels. What set the caravans rolling? A curious, satanic restlessness; some blind glory of the human soul that dared the darkness.

Beyond the coastal plains were hardwood forests and smooth-topped mountains stretching to lakes that were inland oceans. But that was not the half of it. There were the grieving plains, the cactus-crusted deserts, canyons and valleys and Rockies; then another green forest, stretching northward indefinitely. There was too much land to cover with place names. So they blanketed it with a popular slogan: Manifest Destiny.

Generation after generation, the American earth has been our greatest blessing and problem. Many have sensed and said so. But over our national history, three men best conveyed to their times what the earth meant: in the eighteenth century, Thomas Jefferson; in the nineteenth, Frederick Jackson Turner; and in the twentieth, Franklin D. Roosevelt.

Jefferson forged the concepts of democracy and farming into an indissoluble unit. He adopted the French and English physiocratic thinking to the American idiom, molded the idiom into a platform, and erected the oldest political party extant in the Western world today. "The earth," he declared, "is given as a common stock for man to live and labor on." The American farmer was the Atlas on whose shoulders rested the security of the nation and of democracy. Jefferson's Northwest Ordinance opened up 1.5 million fee-simple acres at less than twenty cents an acre. He purchased the whole Mississippi basin and implanted on it the grid pattern that it still retains. Under his leadership, the family farm emerged as the bulwark of liberty.

The historian who made of the agrarian philosophy a philosophy of history, and thus opened the door for rewriting it, was Frederick Jackson Turner. His achievement belongs to the poetry rather than to the science of history. His Frontier Thesis is uniquely American.

Medieval people distrusted nature, that stronghold of Satan, and hid in castles and monastaries. They saw nature as aspiring to the Redemption. In rediscovering man, the Renaissance also rediscovered nature. St. Bernard loved God in spite of this world; Petrarch loved God all the more because of it. Turner carried this tendency forward, equating the fields of the New World with the Garden of Eden. "The master symbol of the garden," Henry Nash Smith points out in *Virgin Land, the American West as Symbol and Myth*, "embraced a cluster of metaphors expressing fecundity, growth, increase, and blissful labor in the earth, all centering about the heroic figure of the idealized frontier farmer armed with that supreme agrarian weapon, the sacred plow." (p. 39)

A son of the Middle Border, Turner lived when American historians centered their writing around either the slavery issue or the Teutonic migration theory. Turner rejected both. He held that the essential history of the New World could be seen by examining not the Atlantic coast but the Great West. To him, the "West" was not only an area; it was a form of society where the cake of custom was broken; a place "where were to be found high faith in man and the will and power to furnish him the opportunity to grow to the full measure of his capacity."[3]

In reaching that full measure, some Americans were willing to turn the sacred plow into a ruthless instrument. The post-Civil War farmer, driven by an expanding market and a contracting conscience, raped the virgin land that Jefferson had acquired and Turner had rhapsodized. This act and its continuation have never been fully comprehended. Pearl Harbor was bombed on a Sunday morning—but the American earth was gutted and mined for decades.

Many doughboys who went "over there" in 1917, to save the soil of France, had wasted America's over here. They left behind rivers running red and brown with topsoil and erosion ruts too wide for leaping. The Europe to which they journeyed had been practicing soil conservation for years. America had played the role of a prodigal son not ready to accept the father's wisdom.

Three of the nine inches of American topsoil have been sacrificed, most of this since the Civil War. Much of the timber has gone too. The spiritual heir of Paul Bunyan was Tom Joad.

With the 1930s came the Dust Bowl. The once-green land

became brown, and it moved—choking and cutting and beating at every living thing. A cloud of dust rose from 1,000 to 15,000 feet, obscuring the sun from the Texas Plains to the Dakotas. Then it started east, until finally, fantastically, ships 300 miles out in the Atlantic reported dust settling on their decks.

It also settled on the desk of the new president in the White House. Franklin D. Roosevelt was not the kind of man to let dust settle. Stirring it up was more to his liking. With him, the agrarian counterattack was launched, and the New Deal was born. He restored America's faith in her ability to control her own destiny and to rescue the landscape. A multitude of alphabet agencies swung into action to restore the lost balance. Gradually, a whole new approach to nature emerged. "For the first time since the trees fell before the settlers' axe," wrote TVA chairman David Lilienthal in *TVA: Democracy on the March* (1944) "America set out to command nature not by defying her, as in that wasteful past, but by understanding and acting upon her first law—the oneness of men and natural resources."

The noble words were often ignored. Throughout the 1940s and into the postwar era, Americans consumed prodigious quantities of nonrenewable resources, leaving less and less for future generations. Every year, there was less per capita to split up, and more among whom to split it. In 1850, the average U.S. square mile supported fewer than eight people. By 1910, that mile was shared by thirty-one. In 1980, even with the addition of Alaska, Americans had to support sixty-two people on the often depleted, gutted, polluted square mile.

This alarming change brought a new word and movement into favor—ecology, from the Greek work *oikos* (household). Coined by Ernst Haeckel in 1869, ecology became a crusading word a century later. Haeckel studied the whole pattern of relations between organisms and their "house," the planet Earth. Eco—ego: I am in the house, I am the problem, I share with everyone else a common planet, a common culture.

Nor is ecology primarily concerned with technological matters. The destruction of fish in the sea and animals on the land has necessitated carrying the fight everywhere.

The basic question is not economic but philosophical. How can we sacralize nature again? How can we make peace with the earth and all that dwells thereon and therein? How can we restore balance in our household?

Ponder such questions carefully. The answers will determine whether or not our culture survives.

With the land comes the lore—that is, the whole body of knowledge possessed by a people. The word itself goes far back into the European past as English *lar*, Dutch *leer*, and German *Lehre* suggest. Chaucer wrote of "Cristes loore" in 1386, and Hernyson a century later:

> Who wil not for shame
> A short tyme suffir lore and lerne?[4]

At that time, "to set to lore" meant to send to school. Teachers were loremasters. Satan, John Milton wrote in 1667, "his lore soon learn'd." He knew that all lores carry us beyond mere history and into the dark places, where rituals, songs, legends, and fantasies are born. Milton and the other great poets who preceded him drew constantly from the "common culture" because they were immersed in it. Their stories, images, and themes were known to most, if not all, of their contemporaries. But who could say this about a twentieth-century poet like Ezra Pound? The great nineteenth-century poet William Wordsworth used the term in "The Tables Turned": "Sweet is the lore which Nature brings. . . ."

In the Romantic Era, lore was linked to such words as animal, bird, and plant. In 1820, London's influential *Gentlemen's Magazine* suggested the suffix "lore" be used instead of the Greek "ology" *birdlore* instead of ornithology, *earthlore* instead of geology, and *starlore* instead of astrology, for instance. Some authors took this suggestion to heart. In the popular Victorian story *Tom Brown's School Days* (1856), Thomas Hughes wrote: "Arthur was initiated into the lore of bird's eggs."

That was a decade after W. J. Thoms coined the term *folk-lore*, the most successful attempt to keep "lore" alive in the English language. No lore predates that of the folk. Egyptian examples of folktales have come to us from the twenty-eighth century before Christ. Early India supplied the *Jatakas* and *Panchatantra*, Arabia the *Thousand and One Nights*, Greece immortal epics and fables. Since folklore is transmitted orally, much of it has been lost, transformed, or adapted. In his great study, *Legend of Perseus*, E. S. Hartland summarizes years of work on the origin of the folktale and concludes that, in the end, his problem is insoluble.

Thoms was not so much a problem-solver as a collector. His goal was to preserve that which was rapidly vanishing, to record the traditional learning of the uncultured classes of civilized nations. Folklore was adopted in many foreign languages and became in German *Volkskunde*. There was an important difference. From the start, Thoms's "folklore" was lore or learning *of* the folk, while *Volkskunde* was *about* the folk. The continual concern with folklore, and its resurgence in the twentieth century, is one of the most hopeful parts of the human story.

To say that folklore is dead is to misunderstand its nature and function. It can and does assume every conceivable form, as time and place demand. Like Proteus in Homer's *Odyssey*, folklore takes "all manner of shapes of things that creep upon the earth, of water likewise, and of fierce fires burning." People who have a folklore never agonize over . . . definitions.

But since we need to define, let us note that the *Dictionary of Folklore, Mythology and Legend* lists twenty-one definitions. Key words are oral transmission, tradition, survival, and communal. Folklore is found most often among isolated groups that maintain their own distinctions and points of reference. This isolation may be spatial, occupational, religious, racial, or linguistic. Folk cultures are essentially rural and religious. Behavior is traditional and personal. The sacred prevails over the secular. All folklore is orally transmitted, but not all that is orally transmitted is folklore.

Hence, folklore is the soil in which later cultural development is rooted. "The vitality of life does not come from the top to the bottom, but like a great tree from the soil up," Woodrow Wilson wrote in *The New Freedom* (p. 81). The point is crucial for anyone studying current cultural movements. Go deep enough and you find not only rich native soil but also a whole substratum brought over from other parts of the world. America is a young nation with old memories.

Yet she has no "national folklore." Literacy became widespread before a true "folk culture" could develop. Waves and waves of immigrants inhibited uniquely American material—here too the melting pot prevailed.

Because folklore flourishes where education and literacy languish, the American South was long a New World seedbed. Here was a traditional society—rural, conservative, hierarchical. Tales of animals and "critters" were common in the backwoods and hamlets of Dixie. They still are.

James Audubon encountered them in the bayous, Opie Read in the mountains, Mark Twain along the rivers. Northern children with southern antecedents heard them too. In his *Autobiography*, Theodore Roosevelt tells how his Aunt Anna and Mother used to entertain him by the hour with tales of life on the Georgia plantations; of hunting fox, deer, and wildcat; and of the queer goings on in the Negro quarters. He was brought up on them.

Folktales of the Negroes and the Cherokee Indians intermingled. In *Myths of the Cherokees*, James Mooney reports that the Great White Rabbit is the hero-god, trickster, and wonder-worker of many tribes. The Indians regarded the rabbit as the fitting type of defenseless weakness, protected and made safe by constant vigilance. Thus, many southern stories now cherished by whites were preserved orally by black and red men.

Those oral treasures were turned into literature by the great preserver of lore, Joel Chandler Harris. His tales are ostensibly for children, but Harris never read or told them to his own children. They were, he openly admitted, allegories. His ten volumes of Uncle Remus stories are southern lore at its best, growing out of the land and the people. They are also monuments to poetic justice and mystery. We watch Brer Rabbit going to sunset prayer meeting to get himself freshened with the Lord, Brer Fox out of sheer compassion providing Brer Rabbit with firewood, Brer Hawk soaring up to say "howdy" to the sun.

On such sound material is erected the myth of the Old South, shining and golden. In it the region is, first and foremost, a land of enchantment. Novels and folktales are convincing ways of depicting it. While historians check each meticulous date, creative artists capture with a few bold and bright colors the feeling and motivation of past glory.

We err in considering myths untrue renditions of the past. If not built on at least a partial framework of historical truth, they will not survive. Most myths are closer to half-formulated beliefs than to facts. As Ortega y Gasset points out in *Ideas y Creencias,* such beliefs rightly claim a position for historians on a par with that of ideas. The study of ideas is not merely the exposition of theoretical views; it is also "the history of the deformations undergone by these ideas when other men adopt them, and also the history of the half-conscious beliefs into which ideas first clearly conceived by the few promptly transform themselves."[4] Mythology is psychology misread as history, biography, or cosmology.

The medievalists had their saints, the British their empire, the *philosophes* their reason. America had incredible diversity (cultural, ethnic, geographic) and pockets of genuine folk culture. But not until the twentieth century did a unique style appear. Entering that century first (which is why, Gertrude Stein said, America is the oldest nation on earth), we found a new mode of expression. Embodying aspects of folklore, and chunks of fakelore, it was an international style adapted to the new electronic environment. Few American folklorists had either the training or the inclination to study it. Learning little from the anthropologists, who made great strides forward in the years after World War II, many professional folklorists did business as usual. As folk material in rural hamlets disappeared, they saw dark days ahead. They lamented the disappearance of zithers but did not hail electric guitars, which took over with a vengeance. Folklore's plight is reflected in the pronouncements of Richard Dorson, a combative scholar and academic who laments:

> The cavernous maw of the mass media gobbled up endless chunks of folksiness, and a new rationale appeared for the folklorist: his mission is to polish up, revamp, and distribute folklore

to the American people. . . . We cannot tarry with folklore performers and popularizers. . . .[5]

Nor can common culture tarry with the Richard Dorsons, who
evolve as does the society they mirror. "Popularizers" do not
threaten folklore; they provide material, arguments, trends.
In their own day, Homer, Dante, and Shakespeare were popularizers. Their spiritual descendants appear on film and tape
today, shaping and leading the new media. They and their
followers—not the folklorists—keep common culture alive.

We need a new breed of scholars whose speciality is not in
examining quaint colorful vestigial remains ("Corncob Pipes in
Central Kentucky . . ." or "Use of Dipthongs in Delta Speech
Patterns") but in following the changes and adaptations of
mainline common culture. This new breed would find clues in
our literary masters. Walt Whitman's *New World Metaphysics*
would be central. So would the *Journals* of Ralph Waldo Emerson
and of Henry David Thoreau, who loved "the music of the
telegraph wires." They would explore our national obsession
with literalism through ten generations of art. They would ask
why European man-made objects tend to look like cells, while
those made in America look like crystals. In short, these new
scholars would ask basic questions which elitists have ignored.

The dilemma of such innovators is obvious: they are literate,
self-conscious elitists themselves, trying to cope with people
whose attitudes, values, hopes, and fears are different from their
own. Peter Burke, one of our best theorists, states the problem
in the first chapter of *Popular Culture in Early Modern Europe*:

> We want to know about performances, but what have survived
> are texts. We want to see performances through eyes of insiders,
> but are forced to see them through the eyes of literate outsiders.

Yet good work and new methods are appearing, especially in
the "folklife movement." Adapted from Swedish *folkliv*, the
emphasis is on folk culture in its entirety. By limiting themselves largely to literary aspects of folklore, scholars have
tended to slight all other aspects and to take the material studies

out of context. In Sweden today, over 400 communities maintain "outdoor museums." The first such venture in America was in Decorah, Iowa, in 1925. The most spectacular is Williamsburg, Virginia (begun in 1926 and still going strong). Despite good work at Cooperstown, New York; Sturbridge, Massachusetts; Shelburne, Vermont; and Dearborn, Michigan, we still know and see far too little of folklife. Don Yoder, a leading advocate of the movement, lists things to study: folk names, agriculture, architecture, cookery, costume, crafts, medicine, music, recreation, religion, speech, transportation, the folk year. Back to the plow and the flail, the husking peg and hominy block, the schoolhouse and meetinghouse!

Knowing more about settlement patterns, games, songs, dance, clothing, and customary behavior, we might see folklore as an integral part of the total range of traditional behavior— and hence of common culture.

To illustrate: long-isolated Scotch-Irish farmers in the Ozarks are so deeply Calvinistic that in mixed company they still refer to bulls as "gentlemen cows." Yet they send maidens to dance in apple orchards each spring and encourage couples to "jolly themselves" in newly planted fields, thus helping seeds to germinate. In the ritual for sowing flax, Vance Randolph reports, the farmer and his wife appear naked in the field at sunup. The woman walks ahead as the man sows. They chant a rhyme that ends, "Up to my ass, and higher too!" Every few steps, the man throws seeds against the woman's buttocks, singing and scattering until the planting is done. "Then they just lay down on the ground and have a good time," Vance concludes. A less delicate informer has this to say of turnip planting:

> The boy throwed all the seed, and the gals kept a-hollering "Pecker deep! Pecker deep!" And when they got done, the whole bunch would roll in the dust like wild animals. Ain't no sense to it, but they always raised the best turnips on the creek!

There are many variations and deviations of folklore. Folklore comes from the soil, springlore from the water. Springlore is a variant of waterlore, which flows in all cultures. Water is ritualistic, working in two ways: it gives and it takes away. It gives happiness, health, wisdom; it takes away pain, evil, and the grime of life. For centuries, people have gone to natural baths and springs to find out who they were, to regain the lost laughter of infancy. For a while, the automobile and airplane threatened to make most of America's great springs and watering places outmoded, but as the twentieth century ends, they are having a notable revival.[6]

Folklore is the country mouse talking, and he delights us. But what of his cousin, the city mouse? Taken to the city, twisted to make a fast dollar, folklore can become fakelore. Nor does the story end there. Taking genuine urban material, created for mass consumption, artists and admen are creating a body of material that is as true to its environment as folklore was to the rural one. We can label it poplore, and it also deserves a place in our lore-analysis.

Imitating genuine ballads and folktales (if that is the essence of fakelore) is no new enterprise. Elite artists as respected as William Wordsworth, Heinrich Heine, and Christina Rossetti all tried it, but they wanted their imitations to be accepted as literature. The people who "made up" Paul Bunyan, on the other hand, tried to pass him off as a genuine folk hero, created by oral tradition.

The poet Carl Sandburg asserted that the folk had invented Paul Bunyan, so that this remarkable and authentic creature was in fact as old as the hills, young as the alphabet. Actually, the Paul most Americans knew was younger than Sandburg's *Chicago Poems*.

A plethora of phony folk heroes and villains flooded our books, movies, and television screens. *Life* published a "remarkable new series" (starting in August 1959) on "The Folklore of America," which was mainly fakelore. Pecos Bill did not come from the Wild West but from the typewriter of Edward ("Tex") O'Reilly. Annie Christmas's spicy saga can be traced not to the New Orleans brothels but to the typewriter of Lyle Saxon. Margaret Montague dreamed up Tony Beaver. Daddy Joe was contrived by Stewart Holbrook, Big Mose by Herbert Asbury, Whiskey Jack by Charles Brown, and Strap Buckner by Florence Barns. Jeremiah Jones refined fakelore by combining the appeal of sailors and cowboys—his "Bowleg Bill" specialized in riding giant tunas. "Maybe the scholars have been following a false lead," Bernard De Voto wrote in *Harper's* for June, 1955. "Maybe popular literature isn't a folk art at all." By then factory-made folklore had blazed a trail across American journalism, advertising, and entertainment like a jet plane racing across a cloudless blue sky.

One of the first writers to deal with the consequences of this was Walter Lippmann. As early as 1922, in *Public Opinion*, he gave examples of "oversimplified patterns" in American life that gave us ways to defend our prejudices by seeming to give definitiveness and consistency to our daily experience. For years thereafter, Lippmann pointed to pseudo events (the fakelore of journalism) that "ignore the world outside and concentrate on the pictures in our heads." In so doing, Lippmann piqued most of the master imagemakers. It remained for Daniel Boorstin, in *The Image. Or What Happened to the American Dream* (1962), to dissect a pseudo event: (1) it is not spontaneous, but planned and planted; (2) it is planted to be reported and reproduced; and (3) it is tied in with a self-fulfilling prophecy.

Fakelore is to folklore what the pseudo event is to the real event. And thus the emergence, in the Eisenhower years, of a new Gresham's law of American public life: counterfeit happenings will always drive spontaneous happenings out of circulation. Poison tastes so sweet that it spoils our appetite for plain food. When the gods want to punish us, they make us believe our own advertising.

In such a climate, folk songs ran in out of the hot noonday sun to the air-conditioned comfort of nightclubs. The authentic folk-song style—with its austere, high-pitched melody—was turned into something sentimental and sweet. To put it bluntly, the guts were removed from folk music. Alan Lomax, a leading folk song collector, noticed that when Aunt Molly Jackson sang to country folks in Oklahoma they called it the most beautiful music they had ever heard. When she repeated the program for city children, they compared her singing to a cat's yowling.

To the first audience, the folk "gapped-scale" and modal intervals were still familiar; to the second, raised on mass media kitsch, one had to adjust the intervals, remove the harshness, and electrify the guitar. Folk songs became pop songs.

But the music and lore of the Elvis Presley era dwelt in a strange no-man's land. It aped and honored the old folk idiom and metaphor, like the suburban "colonial home" that had a fireplace, spinning wheel, and picket fence—complete with electric stove, sewing machine, and television. No one summed up this cultural schizophrenia better than Marshall McLuhan in *Understanding Media*:

> The past went that-a-way. When faced with a new situation, we tend always to attach ourselves to the objects, to the flavor of the most recent past. We look at the present through a rear-view mirror. We march backwards into the future. Suburbia lives imaginatively in Bonanzaland.

What McLuhan had done was study folklore, discern and reject fakelore, then discover poplore. He had, in a single lifetime, gone through the whole cycle I am trying to describe and document.

The new poplore is not the antithesis of traditional folklore. Pop is not slick but savage; in musical terms, it avoids the chromatic scales of the nightclub and uses the old Greek musical modes. Both folklore and poplore avoid sentimentality; reject the "arty" approach for the earthy; draw from primary materials, colors, and emotions. The line of force connects more with the stomach than with the cerebellum.

The world has changed, and the young are moving out into realms their parents will never enter. The young have always done this, only to return and occupy the stable, conservative positions they once decried.

The folk-fake-pop division is no neat thing; bits of data do not fit the pattern. Much genuine folklore and folk music remains, for example, in distant valleys. Perhaps factories and computer centers will create a new vigorous folklore of their own; the notion that folklore is dying out is itself a kind of folklore.

Poplore may lack both the vitality and the significance I attribute to it—only time will tell. But from the information available at this moment, I believe that Andy Warhol, James Rosenquist, Claes Oldenburg, and George Segal changed the course of American art. We will continue to enjoy Molière, Shakespeare, and Ibsen, but now that we have witnessed ''happenings,'' the theater will never be the same.

The performing arts have found a way to be involved in modern life and to speak its idiom. Having been dominated by classical forms and European models for decades, they broke out in the 1960s, as traditional lines and barriers were pushed aside. Instead of scripts, actors ad-libbed. A kaleidoscopic variety of subforms sprang up in the arts, and the street itself became a stage. This was the world of *poplore*. Some of it, the artificial and pretentious, passed quickly from the scene. But like every lore, it left its mark. Probably only *10 percent* of it will survive. But can we ignore gold nuggets because they are found amid tons of fool's gold?

Power plus structure equals a life of being. The poplore that sprang to life was pointing to something much larger than publicity—perhaps to a new ontology. We are much too close to put forth any final judgment. We can only record some manifestations and let history take over:

FOLK	FAKE	POP
oral	verbal	multisensory
traditional	nostalgic	experimental
realistic	romantic	psychedelic
earthy	sticky	tart
homespun	factory-spun	polyester
continuity	transition	explosion
improvised	ersatz	electronic
cowboy	Buffalo Bill	Bonanzaland
community sing	folk festival	Disneyland

One land, three lores: or is it a case of three in one? Beneath the surface, aren't folk, fake, and pop part of the same tradition? What do they have in common? In the days ahead, these are the questions we must answer.

NOTES

1. See Mircea Eliade, *Cosmos and History: The Myth of the Eternal Return* (New York: Harper, 1954), for a fuller development of this line of thought.

2. For a summary, see Robert E. Riegel, "American Frontier Theory," *Cahiers d'Histoire Mondiale* 3 (1956), and Henry Nash Smith, *Virgin Land, the American West as Symbol and Myth* (Cambridge, Mass.: Harvard University Press, 1950).

3. In *Frontier: American Literature and the American West* (Princeton, 1965), Edwin Fussell tries to show how the frontier "passed into American culture and became a formal principle in our literature."

4. See section on "Lore" in *The Compact Edition of the Oxford English Dictionary* (Oxford: Oxford University Press, 1971), vol. 1, p. 444.

5. Henri Peyre, "The Influence of Eighteenth Century Ideas on the French Revolution," *Journal of the History of Ideas* 10 (1949): 345.

6. Richard Dorson, *Folklore Research Around the World* (Bloomington: University of Indiana Press, 1961), summarizes the matter. See also Alan Dundes, *The Study of Folklore* (Englewood Cliffs, N.J.: Prentice-Hall, 1965).

7. See Marshall Fishwick, *Springlore in Virginia* (Bowling Green, Ohio: Popular Press, 1979).

FURTHER READING

Carstensen, Vernon, ed. *The Public Lands* (New York: Holt, 1959).

Dorson, Richard. *American Folklore and the Historian* (Chicago: University of Chicago Press, 1971).

Ekirch, Arthur A., Jr. *Man and Nature in America* (New York: Columbia University Press, 1963).

Heinlein, Robert A. *The Green Hills of Earth* (New York: New American Library, 1980).

Randolph, Vance. *Pissing in the Snow and Other Ozark Folktales* (Urbana: University of Illinois Press, 1977).

Spectorsky, A. C. *The Book of the Earth* (New York: Macmillan, 1957).

Tichi, Cecelia. *New World, New Earth: Environmental Reform in American Literature from the Puritans through Whitman* (New Haven: Yale University Press, 1979).

Twelve Southerners. *I'll Take My Stand: The South and the Agrarian Tradition* (New York: Appleton, 1930).

5
MYTHS AND DREAMS

Not only is God dead, but try
getting a plumber on week-ends.

Woody Allen

People live by the mythology of their time. Every age is credulous
in its own way. How could distant ancestors ever believe that
heaven and earth were made out of a broken egg, heaven being
the shell, earth the yolk, ocean the surrounding fluid? That rain
clouds were cows with full udders, waiting to be milked by the
wind of heaven? Or (in the Middle Ages) that angels danced on
the heads of pins, children could win crusades, and hell was a
real place? Or (moving to Bull Moose days) that Negroes were
inherently inferior, progress was inevitable, and imperialism
was a Christian duty? We must not be too smug. One day some-

one will be asking, "Did you *really* believe that you were splitting atoms and that the absurdity you subjected children to was education?"

Myths describe and illustrate deep structures of reality. They use imagery to express the eternal in terms of the temporal. All religions depend on myth. Any sentence that contains an absolute ends up with mythic overtones. The only nonsymbolic thing we can say about God is that He is symbolic.

True places are not found on maps. They are reached not by roads but by insights. At the heart of art, literature, and culture are myths, metaphors, archetypes, and folklore. We have given up the old labels—fairy tales, sagas, romances, ballads—but not the old yearnings and hungers. We go, whenever we can, to the Garden of Delight and pick the priceless fruit from the golden bough.

Sages understand this. Mythology is transformed into history; history into folklore; folklore into literature. Concepts and emotions are molded into images, creeds, and crusades. Plato's Ideas, Kant's Categories, Goethe's Mothers, Jung's Archetypes, and McLuhan's Media are illustrations. Whenever we reach the point where abstract rationalization can go no farther, myths take over. We draw from our still unspent and yet unexhausted past.[1]

The history of ideas is both the exposition of theory and the record of the deformations undergone by men's ideas; the history of half-conscious beliefs into which ideas conceived by the few transform themselves into general currency. "I find it easier to believe in a myth of gods and demons than in one of hypostatised abstract nouns," C. S. Lewis writes in *The Problem of Pain*. "And after all, our mythology may be nearer to literal truth than we suppose."

Many nonreligious Americans are trinitarians: they believe in mechanism, militarism, and money. Promethean by nature, proud of stealing the fire from heaven, they challenge all the rules. So important are the things close at hand—nothing pleases them like practicality—they have gone into space to subdue the infinite. Infinity, as other ages understood the word, signified the godhead of the world whose creator was unbounded.

Myths are expressions of concern about our place in the cosmos and our relation to our neighbors. They are not hypotheses, but integrating ideas. They may be so much a "part of our culture" that we learn them not in church or school, but in our everyday life and conversation. Many Americans still believe in the "rags to riches" myth, which flourished in colonial times. Our myths are created primarily in the area of economics and politics, amplified by the mass media. Belief in them, Herbert Muller points out in *The Uses of the Past*, "strengthens our faith in ourselves and helps to maintain the habits of enterprise and self-reliance."

One best-selling American writer built his career around telling and retelling the basic American myth of success: Horatio Alger, Jr. He turned out 135 novels that sold over 20 million copies. "Writing in the same vein becomes a habit, like sleeping on the right side," he admitted. "Try to sleep on the left side and the main purpose is defeated—one stays awake."

He restated the basic and sacred American success myth, with minor variations, time and again:

> I am a poor but sturdy lad in the cruel city. I shall get ahead, for I have pluck and luck. That is why they call me Plucky Pete (or, for variety, Tattered Tom, Ragged Dick, or Lightning Luke).
>
> My father is dead and my mother takes in washing. Still I work hard, live clean, and wait for my break. I know that virtue is its own reward—but also that God helps those that help themselves. My break comes. I find a lost wallet, return it to Rich Man, and get my reward—a dime. I also get a smile from Rich Man's daughter (she is a beautiful Anglo-Saxon blonde) and the chance to start at the Bottom of the Ladder. This will allow me to help mother, and get along in the real world of business.
>
> There is a slick mustached man in the office who expects to take over the blonde and the business. But by pluck and luck I discover that he's a secret swindler. A fistfight occurs but I win. (I live clean – he smokes.) I get the business, the girl, and enough money to make mother safe for life. We all live happy ever after.

Silly? Oversimplified? Of course. But Alger's millions of readers could and did take these little moral stories seriously.

We still do. *The Right Stuff*, Tom Wolfe's 1979 best-seller on the astronauts, has different words, but it is still the same old tune.

To Americans then and now, success partakes of a mythology connected with the flag, the Constitution, the car, the credit card, and the better job. It is all true because newspapers and magazines provide documentary evidence. Thomas Edison started as a newsboy, Adolph Ochs as a printer's devil, Andrew Carnegie as a messenger. Henry Ford started as a night fireman, and John D. Rockefeller roamed the countryside looking for a job. Ray Kroc was a down-at-the-heels salesman when he took over McDonald's. And as for the astronauts—they really DID get to the moon. All this—with a little pluck and luck.[2]

The best examplar in politics in Abraham Lincoln. This humble rail-splitter saved the Union and, in the Lincoln Memorial, broods over the nation, a mythic demigod. Many other presidents were poor boys, enjoying none of the education and affluence of upper-class America. A recent example is Harry Truman. Turned down when he applied to West Point, he served as timekeeper for a railroad and wrapped papers for the *Kansas City Star*. His men's clothing store in Kansas City failed, but he kept on climbing. Finally, he got to the White House, where he put a sign on his desk: "The buck stops here." He had the strength and confidence not only to lead but also to command. The American success myth was still working.

But not for Horatio Alger himself. None of the success he described for millions of readers spilled over into his own life. A love affair with a married woman, family antagonism, and a haunting fear of failure almost destroyed him. At the end, he wrote steadily, desperately, pursued by demons. When he died, it was easy to parody his life in an epitaph:

> Six feet underground reposes Horatio Alger, Helping Himself to a part of the earth—Struggling Upward and Bound to Rise. He hopes to be On Top, where all can say he has Risen from the Ranks.

When Horatio Alger's writing went out of date, others took over. Elbert Hubbard wrote a little moral piece called "A Message to Garcia" in 1889. George Daniels of the New York

Central Railroad distributed over 1.5 million copies. Translated into Russian, French, German, and other languages, Hubbard's "Message" became a way of spreading American mythology around the world. By that time, Hollywood was ready to take over.

Hollywood, one of the key spots for American mythology, is a suburb of Los Angeles in southern California, but it is much more. Hollywood is the world's dream factory and escape hatch to Never Never Land.

The basic inventions that made images move came from Europe and the New Jersey laboratory of Thomas Edison. First, there were kinetoscopes, peepshows, and nickelodeons. In 1891, Edison applied for patents on both the camera and the projector, which made possible the first successful picture arcade. It opened in New York City in 1894.

Capitalizing on the ever-popular theme of sex (typical titles were *The Gaities of Divorce, Who's in My Bedroom?* and *The Maid's Guest*), the craze spread rapidly. By 1909, there were between 8,000 and 10,000 movie theaters in the country.

The industry began to concentrate in Hollywood, where the weather was ideal for shooting. In the next decade, the new moviemakers developed nine major categories from popular drama and fiction: epic spectacular, adventure romance, farce, melodrama, problem play, love story, classic, mystery crime, and Western. The last seemed from the very beginning to be most "American" and to satisfy the widest audience. Long after the automobile came, people liked to imagine themselves on horseback.

The Great Train Robbery (1903) was the first motion picture in the modern sense. Governed by a single story line, it combined the techniques of directing, editing, cutting, and filming known at that time. It also introduced "Broncho Billy" Anderson, the screen's first cowboy hero.

Films synthesize literature, drama, music, painting, dance, and photography. They blend time, space, and memory into immediate projection; what we see is not so much a *product* as a *synthesis*.[3]

During the Great Depression, mass production stopped in

many factory towns, but not in Hollywood. The 1930s and 1940s seem, in retrospect, the Golden Age BT (Before Television). In terms of popular success and themes, few directors have matched the achievement of Frank Capra, who, between 1936 and 1939, produced four movies that caught the essence of that era: *Mr Deeds Goes to Town, Lost Horizon, You Can't Take It with You,* and *Mr. Smith Goes to Washington.* The message went out to the world. It still does.

Before and especially during World War II, Hollywood was both a movie factory and a myth factory. Millions of people all over the world had their dreams and fantasies shaped by these movies. Were they not, in the long run, a more potent weapon than the atomic bomb?

Psychologists point out that films (like other major carriers of popular culture) re-create archetypes, which Carl G. Jung defines as involuntary manifestations of unconscious processes, whose meaning can only be inferred. Archetypes appear in myths and in dreams. We yearn to escape from our narrow bonds, to find sanction and consecration. The lives of the hippies and flower children do not reflect myths exclusively American but follow a pattern recognizable in older cultures.[4]

In the 1970s, outer space became the chief area of mythmaking. Hollywood picked up the beat, producing such film successes as *Star Wars.* Gene Roddenberry, creator of television's *Star Trek,* called it " 'Wagon Train' to the stars," emphasizing the similarity to the Westerns that had been popular since 1903. Movement is still the main motif, made explicit in the new films in the flyby of the starship. The stories of space are really about our heritage. They give us our past as our future, while making our present the past. Commenting on this time-trick, William Tyrrell has said:

> Myths no longer link us to the past, since we know the past is gone and is of historical, not immediate, relevance to the present. Science fiction disguises our past as our future—not the historical past but the mythic past of our first beginnings.[5]

We have a multimythology—perhaps because we have processed and acculturated more people than any other modern nation. To do this quickly, we have had to invent and embellish symbols, slogans, and myths. "Americanization" has become in itself a mythic process.

Although millions of immigrants became "American," they did not leave primordial memories on the dock. What they brought, both physically and mentally, is the essence of our nation. The Italians not only imported their pizzalore, but they also turned it into the great American eatout. The hamburger may have originated in Hamburg, Germany, but it has become the essence of our fast-food culture. The same can be said for French fries and other items from around the globe.

Are the old myths gone, or have we clothed them in space suits and sent them into orbit? Are the gods dead—or have they assumed new roles and voices? Look around and see for yourself.

To understand myths—however presented—we must understand the men who make them and the media that convey them. Film, radio, and television scripts comprise a new form of literature that must be studied alongside poetry, drama, and fiction.[6] How many people can name *any* television writers? Know that Nat Hiken wrote the *Sergeant Bilko Show*, which stands with the best comedy writing, or know that Earl Hamner did *The Waltons,* turning the University of Virginia into Boatwright but leaving the Blue Ridge much as it seems to myriads of tourists, or know that Gene Rodenberry's *Star Trek* scripts have already become "classics"? In twenty years, television has changed our cosmology. Earth, air, fire, and water have lost their place as simple absolutes. Space, time, energy, and mass are now basic—and all are shaped by videoculture. No one who studies or teaches can ignore this central fact.

"Nonsense," you may say. "The boob tube has nothing to offer. All it does it put me to sleep."

"To sleep, perchance to dream; ay, there's the rub."

For might not television be a nonlinear collective dream for our whole society? Does not the strangely seductive iconic tube induce a special *kind* of sleep, one that puts us into dream world wide awake?

Note the striking similarity between television and dreams.[7] Both are visual, highly symbolic, involve multiple fantasies. Both contain much that is trivial and nonsequential—but in the long run form a mosaic that makes sense at a greater distance. Television, like dreams, is full of "avoidance mechanisms," many built in unknowingly by the Federal Communications Commission. By *not* showing us things for the *outer* eye, we create them more strongly with the *inner* eye. Imagination hangs on after observation has faded away.

The mirror on our wall is both Alice's looking glass and the television screen. Our electric wonderland is our dreamland, so much a part of us that there is little rational comprehension.

Today, *cinema* dreams lack the penetrating power of *television* dreams. We become a star on the big screen; on the small one, we become the role. There, in our own living rooms, we ARE the stuff that dreams are made of.

Do we shape television more than it shapes us? Not just by rating and buying products, but by dreaming? Does a television society create its own interior video world—purposefully and subliminally—then react to it?

In *General Introduction to Psychoanalysis* (1924), Sigmund Freud wrote that many of our wishes were transformed into dreams through four processes: condensation, displacement, inversion, dramatization. The parallel to television is inescapable. These steps apply not only to dreams but also to nightmares. What happens when the dream goes amuck?

The power of the media delights and often terrifies me. I see in Jerzy Kosinski's *Being There* the key story of my generation. (A child, raised only on television, is so out of touch with reality that he grows up to control the real world.) To have it produced as a comedy, starring Peter Sellers, added a fiendish touch. When the Iranian crisis came and more than fifty Americans were held hostage, I expected the media to keep me abreast. I did not expect that all networks and most national journals would, unceasingly, feature this story over every other story day after day, week after week, beginning at the crack of dawn and recapitulating *after* the eleven PM local news. I began to know more about the Iranian captors than I did about my own students. I saw a president faltering in the polls suddenly rise to new glories—by doing nothing about the hostages but staying on camera. Whether or not military intervention in the Middle East will "save" or "renew" us remains to be seen. We have already seen how the process works, on a more modest scale, in the field of advertising. Consider the case of Seven-Up, the Un-Cola.

By all-out media attacks (including psychedelic frameworks, bright and rapid hallucinogenic images backed by a soundtrack) Seven-Up leaped from obscurity to the "big time" with Coke and Pepsi. The drink did not change: but media magic seemed to transform (as in a dream) the drink, the drinkers, and the environment. In a drug culture, where the need for escape and release was nonnegotiable, those making commercials got into the subconscious. The sales of Seven-Up zoomed. This was not just a soft drink, but a mind-expanding trip. Come on, now— space-out on Seven-Up!

Is *that* any way to run a campaign? Is this the path mythology will take in the years ahead? If so, what kind of global common culture will flourish?

Popular culture is pervasive in itself—literally part of the air we breathe; it is also the mediator through which much of what we have called the Great Tradition (in science, theology, jurisprudence) reaches us. Questions once left to religious myth are now answered in popular entertainment. In terms of their ultimate source and meaning, Harold Schechter argues in *The New Gods: Psyche and Symbol in Popular Culture*, religion and entertainment, instead of being at opposite poles, are closely connected. Not only salesmen and comedians, but evangelists and itinerant popes, use the media to reach their fellow man. A new common culture is forming.

Is it not already central to understanding the myths and dreams of the contemporary world?

NOTES

1. See Wendell C. Beane and William Doty, eds., *Myths, Rites, Symbols: A Mircea Eliade Reader* (New York: Harper & Row, 1975).

2. For a fuller summary, see Moses Rischin, ed., *The American Gospel of Success* (New York: Quadrangle Books, 1965). Self-help books continue to flood the market. Two examples, from the late 1970s: *Your Erroneous Zones* and *I Ain't Much But I'm All I Got*.

3. Of the dozens of books about Hollywood and film, Ezra Goodman's *The Fifty-Year Decline and Fall of Hollywood* (New York: Signet, 1961), and Robert Warshaw's *The Immediate Experience* (Garden City, N.Y.: Doubleday, 1962), provide good overall perspectives.

4. See Harold Schechter, "The Myth of the Eternal Child in Sixties America," in *Popular Culture Reader* (Bowling Green, Ohio: Popular Press, 1978), pp. 64-78.

5. William Tyrrell, "Star Trek as Myth and Television as Mythmaker," in *Popular Culture Reader*, pp. 79-88.

6. The first scholar to put television in this larger context was Erik Barnouw, whose multivolume *History of Broadcasting in the United States* is still standard. His book on *The Sponsor* (Oxford: Oxford University Press, 1979) breaks new ground in exposing pressures on this new art form.

7. These ideas are developed by Peter H. Wood, "Television as Dream," in *American Film*, January 1976. See also Barry Cole, *Television Today: A Close-Up View* (Oxford: Oxford University Press, 1981).

FURTHER READING

Barthes, Roland. *Mythologies* (Paris: Editions du Seuil, 1957).

Beane, Wendell C., and Doty, William, eds. *Myths, Rites, Symbols: A Mircea Eliade Reader* (New York: Harper & Row, 1975).

Cassirer, Ernst. *The Myth of the State* (New Haven, Conn.: Yale University Press, 1946).

Cater, Douglass, and Strickland, Stephen. *TV Violence and the Child: The Evolution and Fate of the Surgeon General's Report* (New York: Russell Sage Foundation, 1975).

Frye, Northrop. *Anatomy of Criticism* (Princeton: Princeton University Press, 1957).

Goffman, Erving. *Frame Analysis* (New York: Harper Colophon, 1974).

Lévi-Strauss, Claude. *The Savage Mind* (Chicago: University of Chicago Press, 1966).

Mehrabian, Albert. *Non-Verbal Communication* (Englewood Cliffs, N.J.: Prentice-Hall, 1973).

Nimmo, Dan D. *Popular Images of Politics* (Englewood Cliffs, N.J.: Prentice-Hall, 1974).

6
THINGS

Things are in the saddle
And ride mankind.

Ralph Waldo Emerson

"I am collecting the history of our people," Henry Ford wrote, "as written into *things* their hands made and used. A piece of machinery or anything that is made is like a book—if you can read it."[1] To read objects is a basic need in any common or popular culture.

Alice discovered that Wonderland was made up of cabbages and kings and a number of things. We too live in a wonderland in which (said Walt Whitman) a mouse is miracle enough to stagger sextillions of infidels. An infinity of things fill the space-time continuum. They determine our lives, our ideas, our thinking. Man the toolmaker wrestles with the raw stuff of life—stone, wood, metal. As he increases in skill and fortitude, he develops a technology; having a technology, so does he have a history. Some of the most vital, subversive, explosive segments we call popular culture.

Objects are the building blocks of reality—sensitive indicators of who we are, where we come from, where we intend to go. Long after an individual has died, and his language and culture have disappeared, artifacts remain. By digging into the earth, archaeologists uncover the past. Things form the solid basis of our understanding and concern for human beings who preceded us. Archaeology plus imagination equals historical insight.

Dynamos, telephones, cameras, film, printing presses, plastic discs, picture tubes: these things are the essence of popular culture—and a new common culture.

The thingness of things has fascinated the liveliest intellects since Aristotle's time. A conscious interest in what Lewis Mumford in *Art and Technics* calls "the go of things" has been a major factor in history, predicated in every period, event, sequence. Yet few people know how to deal with, or even to describe or classify, the artifacts that make things go—things made by man purposefully so that he transforms materials already existing.

Vox populi not only shows what Everyman wants on the television screen, radio station, movie marquee, and billboard, but also in the kitchen, garage, pool hall, and the supermarket. The more prevalent (or popular) the object, the more certain its importance as a cultural cipher. To de-cipher is to find the key to the world in which people actually live. Observe this event: a one hundred pound woman drives a two ton car two blocks to the grocery store. Circling ten minutes to find a parking space, she goes in, buys a loaf of bread, and drives home. Does she know:

1. That the cost of the bread now includes factors like gas consumption and car depreciation?
2. That she has added to problems (such as energy shortage and air pollution) that may bring down our whole nation?

3. That she has missed a chance to walk—one of the few natural exercises left to her by which her body can maintain chemical balance?
4. That she is grossly inefficient since she could have walked to the store and back in half the time?

This episode raises the question of idea-object relationship. Does an object require more time, expense, and attention than it is worth in terms of work or enjoyment? How do cause-and-effect measure the merit of a civilization?

Take another example: toys are among the oldest and most widespread artifacts. They are one of the most important products of popular art. And what of adult toy-play, called hobbies? There are few clues. Ruel Denney's analysis of hot-rodders in *The Astonished Muse* and William Faulkner's account of the American's love affair with his automobile at the close of *Intruder in the Dust* come to mind. So does Luther Gore's study of the waning of interest in model airplanes. A generation ago, model airplanes significantly motivated youth's interest in technology. The experience was a factor in the rapid development of the aircraft industry. In contrast, America's first successful space ventures brought no significant upsurge in hobbies related to aerospace technology. Is "Yankee know-how" in disarray? And does this changing image correlate to the declining youth interest in the building and flying of model airplanes?

Again: what does furniture tell us about the style revolution through which we have lived? Even today's handmade furniture, of traditional material, is devoid of ornament or symbol. There is a conscious effort to break away from historical styles of the nineteenth century—along with a wave of nostalgia. What can this paradox mean?

In the Middle Ages, all experience found philosophical unity and visual form in a single metaphorical system. Such unity and meaning may be found again, in our time. Those seeking it might well ponder the famous epitaph written for Christopher Wren: *si historiam requiris, circumspice* (if you seek history, look around you).

Wren's monuments were, of course, his buildings. Architecture is at the same time the most monumental, social, and popular art. We live, sleep, eat, love, and die in buildings. First we shape them; then they shape us.

We have adapted our buildings to our landscape, psyche, and functions. The log cabin, sod house, frontier lodge, wigwam, adobe are "American." So today are Las Vegas, Disney World, suburbia, Astrodome, and Mall. Is anything more "American" than a filling station? We have put our culture stamp on many structures.

Elitists have decried and denounced it for generations. Leading the parade was Benjamin Latrobe (1764-1820), our first professional architect. He wanted us to copy Europe. So we did, decade after decade. As late as the 1950s, the servile following of Bauhaus and the International style shaped most of America's major buildings. The charm of the village and the coherent small city was swallowed up or disintegrated.

This dismal story was reversed in the 1960s. The same vital explosive culture that transformed art, music, literature, and politics began to put forth a brand new indigenous type of architecture.

One of its early definers and defenders was Robert Venturi, who wrote *Complexity and Contradiction in Architecture* in 1966. He changed "less is more" to "less is a bore." Considering the inhuman qualities of many modern buildings, he wondered if "ugly and ordinary" were not a desirable goal. Joined by his wife/partner Denise Scott-Brown, Venturi published *Learning from Las Vegas* (1972), in which he commented:

> I would say that we are taking a very broadly based thing, the popular culture, and are trying to make it acceptable to an elitist sub-culture—the corporate and governmental decision-makers who hire architects.

Now his ideas are finding support. A new breed of architect began asking questions that had not been raised often. Why do so many shopping malls go "colonial"? How do contractors arrive at design conclusions and for what reasons? How much do the forms seen in films and on television influence real-life

architecture? On what models are popular artifacts and proto-
types built? In what sense can fantasy be "realistic," and how
can such fantasy be embodied in buildings?

The places that have mushroomed most have been studied
least—the service stations, truck stops, and motels. One can
speak of the "motelization of American life," arguing that what
we get on the road we want to bring back into the home. New
suburban neighborhoods seem to be designed for motel users,
with each unit clustered around a private cafeteria. Mom is the
short-order cook; when the kids marry, they set up their own
motel . . . and the beat goes on.

Of course, such an arrangement of things is utilitarian, but it
goes beyond that to speak to the rage for order and for some
kind of community in the midst of Car Culture. Architecture, as
Herbert Read stresses in *The Grass Roots of Art*, is the people's
art. This has long been true, George Coulton adds in *Five Centuries of Religion*. Medieval cathedrals revealed not only the skill
of the craftsmen, but the unity of spirit between craftsmen and
public. Such unity of spirit depends, in part, on icons. America
entered the 1980s short on energy, but not on icons. Indeed, the
craving for external expression of internal conviction (one of the
best definitions of icons) grows as confidence in religion, economics, and politics dwindles. In various phases of the word's
long use and alteration icons have been the most unintelligible
of images: especially in a culture whose visual spectrum is
intense, convoluted, diverse, and ubiquitous. Still, icons do
objectify the deep mythological structure of reality, revealing
basic needs that go from age to age, medium to medium, generation to generation. Cultural ciphers, these admired artifacts help
us to decipher, to unlock the mystery of our attitudes and
assumptions. As objects, they can be approached objectively, but
those who believe in them operate on an emotional level of love
and reverence. The real task is not to define icons but to par-
ticipate in the iconic life.

To do this, one need merely to have a Coke, play a pinball or
slot machine, pick up the telephone, turn on the television,
drive to the corner drugstore. Perhaps your car has a Virgin
Mary on the dashboard—artifact, image, symbol, icon—plastic

piety in the 1980s! Thus do old and new icons converge in our driveways.

Icons accumulate and alter meanings; they also lose them. The iconic Virgin Mary does not speak to the twentieth century as she did to the thirteenth. The swastika does not motivate European youth of the 1980s as it did those of the 1940s. Man carries meanings, not merely objects invested with meanings. The image precedes the idea in the development of human consciousness; the idea drives the image on to glory or oblivion.

In *Icon and Idea*, Herbert Read observes that "thinking in pictures" is the first stage of iconmaking. The ensuing steps to the construction of icons were taken in the prehistoric period. All cultures invent icons. Freud spoke of "optical memory-residues —things as opposed to words." The mind is not so much a debating society as a picture gallery. We look with our eyes, see with our minds, make with our hands. Form and formula fuse. The word becomes flesh and dwells among us.

Icons are symbols and mindmarks. They tie in with myth, legend, values, idols, aspirations. Because of the stress religion places on icons, some would limit icons to conventional religious images typically painted on a wooden panel.² I seek to revitalize the word and relate it to popular culture. Icons still move men, even when they are not recognized as such in supermarkets, discotheques, used car lots, and funeral parlors. They pop up on billboards, magazine covers, and television commercials. Manna may still come from heaven, but much daily information flows through the Big Tube, which constantly flashes images and icons.

Icons traditionally connote fixity and permanence, but pop icons deal with the flux and impermanence of contemporary Protean Man. A style of self-process and simultaneity is emerging: icons adapt accordingly. Objects are the building blocks; ideas are the cement holding them together. Modern man is starved for ideas and objects that give coherence to electric-age culture. What he finds most acceptable, Robert Jay Lifton notes, are "images of a more fragmentary nature than those of past ideologies. These images, though often limited and fleeting, have great influence upon his psychological life."³

With all the changes, icons are still omnipresent. The old process continues: history becomes mythology, mythology begets ritual, ritual demands icons. Concepts end up as creeds. Careers of men as different as Buddha, Christ, Marx, Einstein, and Lenin confirm it. Heroes and icons survive because they function well.

Science "went iconic" with Heisenberg and Bohr—some would say with Plato. Since then, scientists have thought more like poets than technicians. "Thinking in pictures" is the essence of iconmaking, what Freud struggled with for many years. A new generation gets them not from crypts or cathedrals but from billboards and supermarkets. Icons must reflect the change.

A cluster of compatible words emerge—cipher, symbol, artifact, emblem, amulet, totem, allegory, charm, idol, image. Erwin Panofsky's *Studies in Iconology* (1939) begins by defining iconography as "the branch of art history which concerns itself with the subject matter of meaning of works of art, as opposed to their form." Then follows an involved discussion on the distinction between meaning and form. Fourteen pages later, we learn that the act of interpretation requires not only "pre-iconographical analysis in the narrower sense of the word and iconographical interpretation in a deeper sense (iconographical synthesis)." This chapter does not seek its synthesis in such scholarship: instead, it looks at objects of everyday man, convinced that in a democracy, Uncle Sam's icons are by, of, and for Everyman.

Every age is compulsively creative. With each, mythology is transformed into history, history into life, and life into icons. Pop icons are created by and mirrored in all aspects of twentieth-century life.

Religious icons—the most powerful in the past—remain in our secular times. For some, they still have power; for most they are dead. Diedrich Bonhoeffer, German theologian martyred in Hitler's Germany, sensed this when he wrote in *Cost of Discipleship*:

> Honesty demands that we recognize that we must live in the world as if there were no God. And this is just what we do recognize—before God! God himself drives us to this realization. He

makes us know that we must live as men who can get along without Him.

We seem to survive in a world where God is dead. But we cannot exist without images. Living in the Secular City, we crave and create the externalizations of our psychic environment.

Basically, people do not change, and their icons remain essentially the same, as do the purposes to which they are put. Ancient Egyptian tombs were full of icons, religious but also secular. There is a long record of sacred man bearing objects throughout ancient history. Christianity continued the use of iconography. Icons used for prayer abounded in the early days of Christianity. "I have seen a great many portraits of the Saviour, of Peter and of Paul, which have been preserved up to our times," wrote Eusebius, bishop of Caesarea in Cappadocia (c. 260-340). The catacombs were centers of icons, used by both the simple people and the ecclesiastical hierarchy. In Christendom, the meaning and language of icons have always been a strength. Key words were *legend, belief, sacred object, veneration.*

Icons are associated with age and class. They demand a cult, a lore, a spot of veneration. "All sacred things must have their place," Claude Lévi-Strauss notes in *The Savage Mind.* "Being in their place is what makes them sacred. If taken out of their place, even in thought, the entire order of the universe would be destroyed." As the old order has changed, the sacred spots for icons are no longer churches and monasteries but, in the new statements of man's beliefs and aspirations, on superhighways, on television screens, and in discotheques. Still central is their objectification of something near man's essence.

Can we find bases for new definitions and implications deep in the forests of present-day icons? Today, as always, men want to make sense out of the universe. That "sense" must be made in the context of present time, place, and belief. Even "natural" facts, such as birth, growth, and death, are reacted to in a "cultural" fashion.[4] Every style that develops is complete in itself and sui generis, of its own order. Former styles are no longer viable because they are not ours. Iconologically, the consequences are profound and traumatic. They have changed the Great Tradition.

The mainstream of iconology in our time—because of the mass media—is the popular stratum. Elitist critics have long preached that those elements that are esthetically satisfying are aristocratic and for the minority. Other elements—those catering to and acceptable by the majority—are esthetically deficient and contemptible. This condescending attitude is being challenged by such critics as Susan Sontag, who writes in *Against Interpretation*:

> What we are getting is not the demise of art, but a transformation of the function of art. Art, which arose in human society as magical-religious operation, and passed over into a technique for depicting and commenting on secular reality, has in our own time arrogated to itself a new function—neither religious, nor serving a secularized religious function, nor merely secular or profane. . . . Art today is a new kind of instrument, an instrument for modifying consciousness and organizing new modes of sensibility.

Many agree with philosopher Abraham Kaplan: popular art, although not yet arrived at aesthetically great accomplishment has potential and is working toward considerable success.

We could hold up, for example, a grooved plastic disk that we call a "phonograph record." This powerful icon, reproduced by the millions, has changed everything in the music industry and has given a new dimension to multitudes of people around the world (especially the young). Developed originally as a business machine (like the telephone and telegraph), the phonograph (or gramaphone) was available by 1900—and has been both meeting and making public taste ever since.

What the phonograph did was to make music available to anyone, almost anywhere, almost any time. Played on radio stations, records reached millions more (especially in automobiles) who did not even have the machine to play them. Somewhere in all this, the *record*—that plastic disc onto which the music had by some magic been incarnated—took on iconic meaning. Hundreds of new "releases" come out monthly, spin briefly across the scene, and then fall into oblivion. Yet they become part of a new electronic common culture, consuming an incredible amount of time, money, and effort. By what criteria can we judge them? What does the fanatical devotion to phonograph records mean?

We need to devise new criteria and categories for intrinsic meanings. Profiting from Panofsky's work, we should apply the same serious analysis to the current American Renaissance that was used for the Italian and French. This would involve not only surface data (identification, description, authentication) but also interior qualities (evaluation, interpretation, significance).

Most of all, the analysis would involve an intensive reappraisal of the thingness of things. Filling the space-time continuum, haunting our dreams, things determine not only our lives but also our fantasies. Primitive man wrestles with life's raw stuff, stone and wood, until he develops a technology. And as cultures have a technology, so they have a history.[5]

Thus, objects in general, icons in particular, are sensitive indicators of who we are, where we come from, where we intend to go. Long after an individual has died, and even his language and culture, artifacts remain. By digging into the earth, archaeologists uncover the story of the past. Things form the solid basis of our understanding and concern for millions of human beings who preceded us. Archaeology plus imagination equals historical insight.

Ample evidence supports Harold Skramstad's article "American Things: A Neglected Material Culture."[6] Some readers were surprised to find him single out "New Journalist" Tom Wolfe for special praise since Wolfe "demonstrates how insights from a study of new artifact forms are able to increase our understanding of present day American civilization."

More frequently praised is James Harvey Robinson, whose "New History" (now over fifty years old) insisted that we study "not only the written records, but the remains of buildings, pictures, clothing, tools, and ornaments."[7] A promising start was made in the mid-1920s in the twelve-volume *History of American Life* series edited by Arthur M. Schlesinger and Dixon Ryan Fox in which some attention was paid to "non-literary remains and physical survivals." T. J. Wertenbaker's volumes on *The Middle Colonies* and *The Puritan Oligarchy* made use of material culture. But when Caroline F. Ware edited *The Cultural Approach to*

History for the American Historical Association in 1940, neither her introduction nor the thirty-six essays describing the so-called new tools of the cultural historian had a word to say about the historic artifact.

Research Opportunities in American Cultural History (1961) edited by Frances McDermott, calls attention to important possibilities, but none involves a study of artifacts. A look at *Documents in American Civilization* suggests how the historian's idea can be illustrated by an artist, rather than how the work of an artist or artisan can lead the historian to a new idea.

The American Historical Association in 1934 created a Conference on Historic Sites and Monuments and in 1939 added a Special Committee on the Preservation and Restoration of Historic Objects to its standing committee on Historical Source Materials. Both were discontinued in 1947. In 1962, the association tabled a motion to create a new committee on historic sites. The only session devoted to material culture as such was at the association's 1964 annual meeting and at the 1972 annual meeting of the Organization of American Historians. *Word*-people do not know how to handle *images* and *icons*. Historians put their chips on words. One measurable result is declining enrollments, mounting unemployment, and a major effort to plead the historian's case: in words.

The iconologist must find a point of significant beginning. This involves not only structure analysis among arts but configurational analysis of the total gestalt. Criticism and scholarship must catch up with performance. Since today's poets and artists are (as they have always been) bearers of a central pattern of sensibility, that pattern must be explored.

More important, our approach to and study of things must be restructured. Common objects can have uncommon significance. Instead of dismissing as "junk" the products of our mechanized, trivialized, and standardized world, we must try to conceive of them as the foundation of a new style, even a new culture.

Does it offend you to think that a television picture tube, a pinball machine, or a plastic Jesus is in the Great Tradition? The Greeks had their mythological metaphors, the Romans their biographical archetypes, the early Christians their hagiography.

They fade into history. But like the snows of yesteryear, they had their season and fulfilled their purposes. Today, our pop icons are standing in place and serving a purpose. They are *us*. In the 1380s, all experience found visual form in a single metaphorical system. Will this be true in the 1980s?

There is another way to ask the question. How does the evidence on myths, dreams, and icons (presented in chapters 5 and 6) relate to our prediction about the rejuvenation of a common culture (presented in chapter 2)? Common culture is, after all, a single metaphorical system. Can the media become as central to us as the church and theology were six centuries ago? I believe they will. The ingredients are here, and circumstances will provide the experience. Once again, Alfred North Whitehead will have proven correct: "The nonsense of today is the truth of tomorrow."

NOTES

1. Henry Ford, *My Life and Works* (New York: Doubleday and Page, 1922), p. 56.

2. See for example, Leonid Ouspensky and Vladimir Lossky, *The Meaning of Icons* (Basel: Otto Walter, 1952).

3. Robert Jay Lifton, "Protean Man," *Partisan Review* (Winter 1968), p. 47. William Zinssen's *Pop Goes America* (New York: Harper & Row, 1966) pursues the same theme.

4. Myron Bloy, *The Crisis of Cultural Change* (1965), defines technology as the "mind-set" that has become the "Objective spirit" of the Western world.

5. This whole area is explored by John A. Kouwenhoven. See *Made in America* (1948), reprinted as *The Arts in Modern American Civilization* (1960).

6. The article, which appeared in the spring 1973 issue of *American Quarterly*, contains a helpful bibliography on material culture.

7. I am indebted here to research and conversation with Dr. E. McClung Fleming, of Winterthur Museum in Winterthur, Delaware.

FURTHER READING

Brown, Curtis F. *Star-Spangled Kitsch* (New York: Universe Books, 1975).

Fishwick, Marshall, and Neil, J. Meredith. *Popular Architecture* (Bowling Green, Ohio: University Popular Press, 1977).

Gowans, Alan. *The Unchanging Arts* (Philadelphia: J. B. Lippincott, 1964).

Kouwenhoven, John A. *Made in America* (New York: Doubleday, 1948).

Rapoport, Amos. *House Form and Culture* (Englewood Cliffs, N.J.: Prentice-Hall, 1969).

7
STYLE

Style, not substance, will be the wave of the future.

Edward Whetmore

There she was: a new actress to dazzle us with a new hairstyle.
Her name was Bo Derek. The 1979 movie (called *10*) was trivial,
but her hairstyle was tremendous. Called "cornrowing," it had
been popular with blacks for a decade. Involving meticulous
braiding and ornamenting, it was an instant style-craze. Crowds
of white women turned up at the Harlem YWCA Beauty Shop,
which specialized in cornrows. A braids-only salon named Le
Braids Cherie opened in Hollywood, and the media tuned in.
Soon salons in large cities (like Pierre Michel's in New York)
were charging up to $500 to set a single chic head. "The style is
an attention-getter and it frees women from setting, brushing,

and constantly fixing their hair," *Newsweek* reported on January 28, 1980. "Hair stylists are predicting that it will be THE look by the summer."

An age-old process inside popular culture was repeating itself. Whatever a culture does or does not have, it must have a style or, more accurately, a whole range of styles. Style is intrinsic, not extrinsic. Derived from ancient shapes and uses, the shape and contour of a story, picture, or costume, style exhibits the spirit and personality of the creator. The mental image of a person's style is the person himself.

Style is a kind of model building. We draw from visual memory and obscure ancestral springs; this stimulates our creativity. If the products evoke a sentimental yearning for archaic styles, we apply the tag "nostalgia." Imitation is always easier than initiation.[1]

Never formed in a vacuum, style uses words, lines, gestures, and objects with which people are familiar. For this reason, not only individuals but also regions, nations, and even continents have "their own style." America's style is rooted in nonconformist Britain but is shaped by many other European styles, as well as those of aboriginal Americans. Try as they might, Europeans changed in the new environment. The land was stronger than the men—it always has been.

Through style, we parcel out space, time, mass, and energy. The law of probability applies. Of all things that *can* occur, those that *do* become "stylish." Style, which depends not only on logic but also on intuition, gives us surprise and delight. Expect the unexpected. That becomes the operating first principle for mannerism, Dada, pop, and camp. They unseat style and mock premises as did the Radical Chic of the 1960s and the Redneck Chic of the 1970s. Who would have expected sophisticated, urbane Americans to emulate the coarse backwoods Redneck? Yet one finds urbanites dressed in imported blue jeans and expensive Frye boots, trying for the "down home" or "country" look. Further manifestations are the obsession with pick-up trucks, dogs, country and western music, and "hard licker." There is the aping of the uneducated on the C. B. radios, and the high rating for such banal television series as *The Dukes of Hazzard*, movies like *Convoy*, and hit tunes like "Redneck in a

Rock 'n' Roll Bar." Entertainers who want to make it in the city go country.

Is he another "white Negro," as Norman Mailer characterized the early hippies—what Steve Young calls (in his song "Renegade Picker") "partly hippy, partly jigger"? These antistyles eventually become styles in their own right and inspire other antistyles. Those who found Dada too stuffy took to pop art; when pop criticism became overly serious, the jokers invented camp.

Their thesis: when something is quite bad, it becomes, by some perverse chemistry, fascinating and irresistible. Instead of admiring only the best, why not the worst? Thus, the Germans made national parks out of Nazi concentration camps. The American government celebrated the centennial of its Civil War by glorifying the Rebels who had set out to destroy the Union. When does irony become absurdity?

Whatever the complications, style springs from a single source —the imagination of a sensitive person. Mozart, Van Gogh, and Judy Garland had style, but died tragically. Walt Disney, Pablo Picasso, and Aristotle Onassis, on the other hand, had style and died millionaires. Success and style are not synonymous. There are hidden Xs that must be put into every equation.

The artist-creator in the world of popular aesthetics is servant to the culture and slave to the market. Yet there is room for the artist-reformer, sometimes as an outsider from the elite tradition, sometimes as an insider who outgrew the restrictions of a popular form. These people Fred Schroeder calls "outlaws." From studying their work, he has developed an *Outlaw Aesthetics*. He speculates in this book over how artist outlaws are converted to inlaws:

> How is it that Jane Austen and Louisa May Alcott rise out of the teenage sentimental novel? How does George Gershwin rise from Tin-Pan Alley, and Duke Ellington from dance-hall entertainment? How do we get from *Astounding Science Fiction* to Kurt Vonnegut, from Hopalong Cassidy to *High Noon*?[2]

Part of the answer lies with individual genius that appeals to the popular aesthetic, which says an artwork is good because it sells and sells because it never places art above audience.

In the world of mass media, individual styles are often sacrificed to "teams" of writers and producers. These style-teams work together so closely that they may develop a communal style of great brilliance and authenticity. An example is Disney Studios: for half a century, this group of writers, artists, filmmakers, and promoters has turned out productions that the world has accepted as the essence of America.

Although he has been long dead, the spirit of Walt Disney lives on. Born near Chicago in 1899, an ambulance driver in World War I, Disney began making animated cartoons in the 1920s. His first triumph was Mickey Mouse, a style-setter if ever there was one. The tie-in with folklore and common culture is interesting. Old folk traditions tell of a magic mouse skin, of mice stronger than mountains and braver than lions, of a mouse that taunted a ferocious bull, and of mice that banded together to bring about justice. All these things Mickey did—against a background of vacuum cleaners, meat grinders, cement mixers, and killer cats. Those who find the modern world intimidating, often overwhelming, empathize with Mickey and his beloved Minnie. Like Charlie Chaplin, they are always on the side of the little guy.

Disney turned the animated cartoon into one of the most popular genres in art history. Technologically, he was sophisticated and innovative. His full-length features, like *Snow White* and *Fantasia*, are monumental achievements. But Mickey remains his masterpiece. Cast in the Aesop genre, Mickey is a moralist. Like characters in all great dramas, he distorts to make real. The little mouse has a logic and style of his own, and the world loves him.

The Disney story has been told often.[3] Walt turned out the first animated cartoon with sound (1928); the first in color (1932); the first full-length feature (1937); the first with stereophonic sound (1940). He created a universe of interchangeable parts, combining the American past and a universal future. In 1955, he opened Disneyland, a seventy-three-acre tract in suburban Los Angeles. In 1971, the larger and more ambitious Disney World opened in Florida, full of electronic devices, mechanical conveniences, industrial hardware, and slogans.

Critics analyzed and damned what they saw (Max Rafferty, Richard Schickel, Louis Marin, William McDonald, Ariel Dorfman, Herbert Schiller, Christopher Finch, and Peter Blake, among others), but the people keep coming.

What attracts them is a cosmology in which they can believe. Main Street, Adventureland, Frontierland, Fantasyland, Tomorrowland—Popular Culture America. Within a few years after opening, Disney World had become a national mecca for tourists—the most successful outdoor theme park in history—a combination of popular style and good management . . . creativity, sentimentality, verisimilitude, and vulgarity. All are present when one walks around Disneyland (alias Cornsville, U.S.A.), with its ersatz emporium, flying elephants, clay *Tyrannosaurus rex* with a two-foot mouthful of six-inch teeth, and a plastic baby elephant that entertains "Jungle Cruise Voyagers" by squirting water into the jaws of a crocodile.

For detailed listings of Disney doings, one need only check the equipment (telescopic lenses, zoom lenses, time-lapse cameras, synchronized cameras, underwater cameras, etc.) used by cameramen-naturalists who spent months in primitive areas, African heat, Alaskan blizzards, and South American jungles to achieve the authenticity Disney craved. The Disney "style," as created by scores of employees, had become not only national but international.

The same team-play takes place constantly in contemporary America, on a smaller scale. No film or television show can be staged without a team. Nor can any opera, ballet, or theatrical event. Take the Broadway hit *Grease*, which in July 1974 passed its one-thousandth performance. During that time the number of people involved with the production had jumped from four to over two hundred and fifty. In addition to national tours, there were shows in London and in Mexico City, where the show was called *Vaselina*. It had become an international enterprise.

In addition to the impact of *Grease* itself, the play helped to ignite a revival of the 1950s. Radio stations began playing 1950s records, old rock stars were revived, and a quickie 1950s movie, *American Graffiti*, grossed millions. The "style-team" that had started with four mushroomed into the thousands.

If Disney and company illustrate the validity of "style team," others show how movements generate their own rhetoric and style. Major examples are the black revolution, women's liberation, gay revolution, and the Woodstock nation. They changed not only the way millions of Americans thought but also how they dressed, talked, ate, exercised. What combination of circumstances can explain the jogging phenomenon? Suddenly, parks, sidewalks, and roads are full of joggers. A 1980 Gallup poll estimated that 23 million Americans jog or run on a regular basis. *Family Health* insisted the number was much larger. By anybody's count, this was a movement affecting life-style. The San Francisco six-mile Bay-to-Breakers race had one hundred runners in 1963, for example, and over 20,000 in 1979. More racers meant more shoes, equipment, books, laws. *New York* magazine estimated that the "running industry" grossed $800 million in 1979, while the whole fitness industry topped $5 billion. With every new style comes the new gadgetry. Store windows were filled with jog-a-lites, radioactive headbands, wrist radios, runner's pendants, digital chronographs, and pulse monitors. The "unquestioned Bible of running" is the magazine *Runner's World*, followed by a host of similar publications: *Marathoner*, *Today's Jogger*, *Yankee Runner*, *Running News*, *Running Times*, *The Runner*, and *Stride On*. Observers could monitor and measure this explosion; who could explain it?

There were changes not only in what Americans read but also in how it was written. The national "literary style" became more experimental and subjective. Changes were both external and internal. The linear blocklike page gave way to a new emphasis on special type, graphics, inversions, injections, and made-up words (mysterioso, trickology, zapped, flaky, Carterized). Those experimenting were said to have "style" and to be "New Journalists." Thus has it always been. When a singer or a writer has style, we can overlook or forgive anything. Who cares what John Denver or Barbra Streisand sings—or what subject Tom Wolfe or Gay Talese choose? "It Ain't Whatcha Do, It's the Way that You Do It."

If style is supremely important, it is also extremely illusive. Those who have style do not often discuss it; those who talk about it do not have it. Success begets countless imitations. If nostalgia in old Virginia works on television (*The Waltons*), why not try Iowa (*Apple's Way*)? If a male slob (Archie Bunker) wins millions of followers, why not a female slob (Maude)? And on and on and on.

The New Journalists repeat styles, attitudes, even vocabulary.[4] One of Tom Wolfe's admired essays, "Las Vegas," begins:

> Hernia, hernia, hernia, hernia, hernia, HERNia, hernia HERNia, hernia, HERNIA hernia HERNIA. . . .

Meaningless repetition? No. A comment from a spaced-out observer mocking the "running singsong" of the roller at a Las Vegas craps table. The "hernia sound," Wolfe continues, "is part of something rare and rather grand: a combination of baroque stimuli [*sic*] that brings to mind the bronze gongs that Louis XIV personally hunted out in the bazaars of Asia Minor. . . ."

Las Vegas (as the movie *Electric Horseman* demonstrates) has become a style center for America: our Versailles. To many, the idea is repulsive. But Versailles is a dead monument, while Las Vegas is full with energy and innovation. Places like Las Vegas have made neon lighting into a full-blown art form. Realizing this, some art schools are now teaching electronics, wiring, and glass blowing. Transformers, laser rays, mercury vapor, and carbon filaments are becoming artist's tools. From the broad world of popular culture, styles flow as from a cornucopia. Understanding them is a difficult and rewarding task.

Styles do not appear in a vacuum or in art books; they spring up as fads, trends, or movements. The main distinction is duration. Fads last only for a season, trends for several years, movements for a number of years or even decades. No one understands the process or the distinction: the how, why, who, and when. Fads are like shooting stars, illuminating the heavens, then falling back into the darkness. They draw exaggerated zeal. Some achieve the dubious distinction of being "crazes." In my lifetime, there were the "crazes" of eating raw goldfish, crowding into telephone booths, and raiding girls' dorms to steal panties.[5] "Each age has its own follies," Emerson wrote, "as its majority is made up of foolish young people."

The Frisbee was a spectacular fad of the 1960s. So were "head shops," featuring kaleidoscopes, prisms, and reflecting disks. "Ocean in a Bottle" became a craze: a clear plastic cylinder filled with a viscous blue fluid.

Look out of a window after a rain, and you might see a rainbow. Style is like a rainbow, seen only briefly, induced by coincidences in nature that no one can predict or invoke. The rainbow entrances us, and we pursue it like pilgrims. All in vain. Even as we get to the place where we thought we saw it, the rainbow vanishes.

NOTES

1. The literature is vast. The work of Heinrich Wolfflin is a prime reference, although the works of Joseph Margolis, Carl A. Friedrich, Manfred Bukofzer, Helmut Hatzfeld, and John Rupert Martin are also important. See George Kubler's brilliant study of the *Shape of Time* (New Haven: Yale University Press, 1962) read in conjunction with Meyer Schapiro's essay on "Style" in A. L. Kroeber's *Antrhopology Today* (Chicago: University of Chicago Press, 1953). See also Wylie Syper, *Four Stages of Renaissance Style* (New York: Wiley, 1955), and Thomas Munro, *Toward Science Aesthetics* (New York: Abrams, 1956).

2. Fred E. H. Schroeder, *Outlaw Aesthetics* (Bowling Green, Ohio: Popular Press, 1977), p. 15.

3. Despite its open hostility, Richard Schickel's *The Disney Version: The Life, Times, Art and Commerce of Walt Disney* (New York: Simon & Schuster, 1968), remains the best single volume. Christopher Finch's *The Art of Walt Disney: From Mickey Mouse to the Magic Kingdoms* (Burbank, Calif.: Disney Productions, 1973), gives the "official" laudatory story. Herbert Schiller explores more sinister aspects in *The Mind Managers* (Boston: Beacon Press, 1973).

4. See Michael Johnson, *The New Journalism* (Lawrence: University of Kansas Press, 1971), and Ronald Weaver, *The Reporter as Artist: A Look at the New Journalism Controversy* (New York: Hastings, 1974).

5. Many more are described by Paul Sann in *Fads, Follies, and Delusions* (New York: Bonanza, 1967).

FURTHER READING

Finch, Christopher. *The Art of Walt Disney: From Mickey Mouse to the Magic Kingdoms* (Burbank, Calif.: Disney Productions, 1973).

Gans, Herbert J. *Popular Culture and High Culture: An Analysis and Evaluation of Taste* (New York: Basic Books, 1974).

Randall, William Pierce. *The History of American Style from 1607 to the Present* (New York: Crown, 1978).

Voigt, David Q. *America Through Baseball* (Chicago: Nelson-Hall, 1976).

8

HEROES

America is a country which has grown by the
leap of one hero past another.

Norman Mailer

By the end of the twentieth century, we may run out of space,
gas, foreign policy, and time. But God forbid that we run out of
heroes.

In the days of Eisenhower the Conqueror, the valleys stood so
thick with corn that they laughed and sang. Content in one such
valley (of Virginia), I wrote of American heroes. That was back
in AD 1958. Ah, yes, I remember it well.

Across the campus was the chapel in which Robert E. Lee lay
buried. The Noble Knight, without blemish, without reproach;
looking back to Washington's crusade to free the colonies,

forward to Eisenhower's crusade to free Europe. Lee had been nobly served by General Jackson (buried in the local cemetery), Eisenhower by General Marshall (trained at the local Virginia Military Institute). Everything fit, snug in the great Chain of Being—way back in AD 1958.

Exit Eisenhower, enter Kennedy. Suddenly, everything was popping: empires, ideologies, arts, ghettoes, populations, platitudes. Cold wars got hot, kids became cool, and God was dead. A counter culture, shouting its barbaric yawp from the rooftops of Academia, was turning periods into question marks.

The heroic style—masquerading as antiheroic—changed too. Ugly became beautiful, odd became even. The key word was neither realistic nor romantic but psychedelic; not oral or verbal but multisensory; not improvised or planned but electronic.

Suddenly, my old crop—not only the eighteenth-century swashbucklers, squires, and cavaliers, but also the nineteenth-century frontiersmen, self-made men, and industrial tycoons—looked archaic. (The "in" words was irrelevant.) Even the presidency looked different when John F. Kennedy occupied it: he was the first president born in the twentieth century, the first to emerge from the political vortex of megalopolis, the first Roman Catholic. Moreover, he refused to be official and corny. Like a good jazz musician, he knew the power of flatting and deflating. When asked how he became a hero against the Japanese during World War II, he answered: "They sank my boat."

Kennedy abhorred sentiment, purple prose, and platitudes. His careful exploitation of mass media was a hallmark: his press conferences were masterpieces of relaxed, confident exposition. Here was the old F.D.R. Fireside Chat adapted for television by Prince Charming.

Kennedy's assassination in 1963 is the crucial event in the heroic history of our generation. Because of the times and technology, Kennedy had a global popularity unlike that of any other president. That he should be killed senselessly by a former U.S. Marine, who was, in turn, killed while millions of viewers watched on television, forms an unbelievable historic episode—a happening. That the whole assassination trauma was almost repeated with Ronald Reagan in 1981 adds to our sense of disbelief.

This sense of the unexpected, the unbelievable, was flavored with a tang of the grotesque. As in a mixed-up movie in which the film runs backward, we found ourselves in 1964 watching Barry Goldwater campaigning for the presidency on horseback. Old-timers who remembered Buffalo Bill were filled with nostalgia. Not so for most Americans. Even a Texas Ranger seemed better than this. Lyndon B. Johnson, the last of the nineteenth century presidents, retained office.

The Johnson years mirror the knotty and perennial American paradoxes: Virgin Land vs. Raped Landscape; Arcadia vs. Grub City; consensus vs. anarchy; citadel vs. caravan. Some sat in, others sold out. A single catalytic agent, Vietnam, changed old-style American military heroes into new-style villains. Caught between the corncob and the computer, Middle America did not know whether to go back to the farm or forward to the moon.

There was no national mourning when a contemporary of John F. Kennedy—Woody Guthrie—died in 1967. Yet Guthrie was a protopopular hero reincarnated in a talented imitator, Bob Dylan, and in Woody's less talented son, Arlo. The ghost of Guthrie, as much as that of Kennedy, haunts us still.

Left alone with his young brother in an Oklahoma shanty, Woody was an orphan of living parents. Most of his life was spent in compulsive, aimless rambling. Yet he left a body of work—over a thousand songs—that document his period. "Some of them are purty dern left-handed," Guthrie admitted. "They are so left wing, I had to write 'em with my left hand and sing 'em with my left tonsil." Along with more learned contemporaries whom he never read nor quoted—the existentialists—Guthrie helped put antihero stage center. So did Norman Mailer, who emerged as a prototype author of his generation. Going through many changes after writing his best-selling novel about World War II (*The Naked and the Dead*), Mailer mirrored the cataclysmic changes that followed. His personal credo, stated in *Advertisements for Myself*, was to encourage his own psychopathic tendencies, and exist in that enormous present that depends neither on memory or planned intention. Shades of Jean Jacques Rousseau and the Noble Savage!

The heroic hobo was popular again. The word, thought to be derived from ho, boy, had been used for a century to describe homeless and penniless vagrants who first traveled the rails, then the roads. Strong backers of the Populist Revolt in the 1890s (did we restage the election of 1896 in 1972?) then of the Wobblies labor movement, the hoboes have long sung their heady, irresponsible songs:

> Hallelujah, I'm a bum!
> Hallelujah, bum again,
> Hallelujah! Bum a handout,
> Revive me again.

The new King of the Road was Jack Kerouac, whose bestseller was called *On the Road*. This errant prodigal son from the Roman Catholic Church went on to write *Dharma Bums, Visions of Gerard,* and *The Subterraneans*. In his wake came the hippies, city and politics oriented, more anxious to do than to write. For them, liberty, equality, and fraternity became turn on, tune in, and drop out. For thousands of Americans "finding myself" meant freaking out. A new vocabulary of drug addiction cropped up. Often their protest was scattered and controllable, but not at the 1968 Chicago Democratic Convention or on the campus of Kent State in Ohio.

Unheroic or antiheroic characters are deeply rooted in history —fool, clown, scapegoat, freak, rebel without a cause, angry young man. But seldom have they been authentic popular American heroes, pushing knights, generals, and moneymakers off stage. Or so it seemed on the surface, but were the old heroes destroyed or transformed? Were we not still entranced by perennial doubts and fears? Are popular heroes—sometimes, like Nanki-Poo in *The Mikado*, disguised as second trombones— brand new or retreads? Do they not reenact old rites of passage: separation, initiation, return? Do they not venture forth still from the world of common dullness to the region of fleeting wonder?

The heroic scene is changing too rapidly and we are too close to it to give answers. We *can* say that changes in media, lifestyle, priorities, ideologies will be reflected in our heroes.

Motion pictures and television confer celebrity, not just on people, but also on art objects, places, ways of life. Everything is visible with the Big Eye; ethnic groups that were once under-viewed are now seen and discussed far out of proportion to their numerical strength in the total culture. Indians and blacks wage large-scale campaigns against traditional American heroes. Writing of "The White Race and Its Heroes" in *Soul on Ice*, Eldridge Cleaver sees more shame than pride in our heroic past, in which venerated Founding Fathers like George Washington and Thomas Jefferson owned scores of black slaves, and in which legal segregation went unchallenged for decades:

> . . . every president since Lincoln connived politically and cyni-cally with the issues affecting the human rights of most American people—these facts weigh heavily upon the hearts of the white youth.

His sneers at Mr. and Mrs. Yesterday have been repeated and echoed. Not only flesh-and-blood writers, but also comic book characters, have altered. Consider Superman. Created in the Depression as an icon, restlessly eager to embrace violent solu-tions, he has become alienated and disillusioned. Standing on top of a skyscraper, looking at antlike humans below, he muses: "For the first time in many years I feel that I'm alone. . . . "

Not even Superman is as alienated as a group chronicled in *Esquire*. Called the Chickenshits, they wore yellow armbands, carried a yellow flag, and played kazoos. When confronted by opposition, they dropped to the floor and crawled out mumbling, "Grovel, grovel, grovel, who are we to ask for power?"[1]

"Ask for it—who wants it?" Joyce Maynard queried in a widely quoted *New York Times* article called, "An 18-Year Old Looks Back on Life" (April 23, 1972). Everyone is raised on nursery rhymes and nonsense stories, she concluded. "But it used to be that when you grew up, the nonsense disappeared. Not for us."

Why scrutinize and lionize the antihero? Because, the argu-ment runs, he enacts the dilemmas and crises of the generation he represents. Thus, Dylan has taken us through politics, drugs, transcendentalism, communes, love. . . . What the hell else can we ask of him?

Or ask of Janis Joplin (1943-1970), our Right-Here-and-Now-Do-It-Baby who tried everything—including suicide? Fashionably famous for her work with a San Francisco group called Big Brother and the Holding Company, she was quoted as saying: "I don't know what happened. I just exploded." Don Heckman called her a study in tension—beads, fringe, and hair streaming in every direction, her hands constantly moving like curiously delicate butterflies; drinking, cursing, crying, sometimes at the same time. She was under thirty when she joined Jean Harlow, James Dean, Jimi Hendrix, and Marilyn Monroe in the Cult of the Early Dead. "Janis designed her own package," her mother concluded, "and the package became the person." Was this one way to echo McLuhan—the medium had become the message? In any case, Janis proved to be an ephemeral star shooting across Pop Heaven. A decade after her death, few young people remember her or her hysterical renditions.

How can there be heroes without heroines? Where in this subject do we accommodate such historic figures as Sarah Moore Grimké, Lucretia Mott, Elizabeth Cady Stanton, Susan B. Anthony, Carrie Catt, and Eleanor Roosevelt? "I ask no favors for my sex," Sarah Grimké wrote in 1838. "All I ask of our brethren is that they take their feet from off our necks." As the Equal Rights Amendment (ERA) sputtered and stalled in the early 1980s, it became clear that the male foot was not easily dislodged.

The relationship between hero and heroine is not clearly defined or understood. The Battle of the Sexes continues unabated.

Some much admired females of our time have paid little attention to women's liberation. For example, Joan Baez has not endorsed either female or black liberation movements, which divide rather than join people. To her, the relevant question is: How do we stop men from murdering each other? Many women have vigorously opposed ERA.

Our world has become fluid instead of static, dominated by images rather than words. Since we have instant information, we expect instant action. Faced with inevitable problems, we look for leaders with instant solutions. In this sense, the hero of the 1970s was a performer (whatever his field). A host of crucial questions follow. Why do we both demand and destroy stars? Is performance always a means, or can it also be an end?

It may be that a generation that is better educated, more sophisticated, more widely traveled, and more exposed to media than any in history will demand and expect more from heroes. Because no highly publicized figure can hide contradictions, shortcomings, and recorded blunders, the old one-dimensional hero or paragon is finished. We have to accept the new crop, warts and all or not at all. Might this be one cause of the antihero trend?

Media exposure tends to make celebrities rather than heroes, or to confuse the two categories. Was the black athlete who began as Cassius Clay, then changed his name to Mohammed Ali, a celebrity or a hero? Alternately a pseudo poet, buffoon, world champion, and special presidential envoy to Africa, Ali defied the old categories. So did Norma Jean Baker (alias Marilyn Monroe), who started as a sex kitten, then became a fashion model, a highly acclaimed actress, and (after suicide in her mid-thirties) a cult figure. Apparently, she wanted to be recognized as herself, not as a celebrity or as an object to arouse the male erotic nerve. Long after her death, she remains one of our most popular and puzzling figures.

Nothing demonstrates the increased power and pervasiveness of electronic media more than a comparison of a Blonde Goddess Celebrity of the 1950s, Marilyn Monroe, to her successor in the 1970s, Farrah Fawcett-Majors. She is the ultimate hype. Coming to Hollywood from Texas in 1966 (she was chosen Most Beautiful Freshman at the University of Texas), Farrah was shaped by publicist David Mirisch, agent Dick Clayton, talent coach Renee Valente, and hairdresser Hugh York. With a hyphenated name, a baroque hairstyle, and a toothy smile, Farrah took off. A spot on a lady-detective series called *Charlie's Angels* exposed her to millions; Farrah had developed "now" talents, like karate, and she wore no bra. Contracts were hastily negotiated for dolls, deodorants, posters, clothes, public appearances, books, autograph parties, television guest shots, magazine covers, cosmetics conferences, and T-shirts. Farrah's Boswell, Pamela Ecker, continues the story:

> When Farrah left "Charlies's Angels," after one phenomenal attention-getting season, she left with commercial contracts, movie contracts, modeling contracts, and hundreds of thousands of dollars' worth of appearance and products contracts. Farrah left her television series with agents, publicists, and managers. She left with lots of publicity, lots of security, and incredible wealth.[2]

She was a celebrity.

By then (1978) being a celebrity meant being everywhere all-at-once. You saw her everywhere because she was a celebrity, and vice versa. Her face, hands, hair, breasts sold everything. They sold because they included her. America was obsessed with Farrah because America knew her . . . she was the most well-known person of all well-known people. She was famous for being famous. For a little while.

Making celebrities is a national obsession. Since 1974, three major magazines (*People, Us,* and *Celebrity*) have been invented to fuel the celebrity boom. They update earlier publications like *Photoplay, Modern Screen, Motion Picture,* and *Modern Movie.* Favorite topics never change—Everyday Life of the Stars, Unhappiness and Infidelity of the Stars, Sex, and the New Morality. Have you heard the latest on—?

How many celebrities are there? It is hard to say—some are gone before you can count them. Earl Blackwell and Cleveland Amory have compiled a *Celebrity Register* with 2,200 brief biographies. Their criterion for inclusion is simple. All you have to do is weigh press clippings.

Sometimes someone who seems to be a genuine hero ends up a celebrity—Charles Lindbergh, for example. Some become celebrities merely by being born—England's Prince Charles or Canada's Dionne quintuplets. Certain names denote wealth or power in their own right. Who would challenge a check signed by a Rockefeller, for example?

People have become celebrities by climbing the sides of buildings or jumping over canyons on motorcycles. There are even those who become celebrities merely by associating with celebrities. Then they can go on television talk shows and let the world see them. Johnny, Merv, Dinah, Dick, Phil, or Tom will host the event. Then their phones will start ringing, and they will be offered the chance to sell panty hose, sleeping pills, and shaving lotion. Who knows how high their stars may rise?

Local culture is replaced by a synthetic media substance. Entertainment is replete with attitude-forming information. Ads not only sell, they shape. Just as the nineteenth century took its toll on the worker's body, so does the twentieth century on his mind. Not the illusion of progress but the illusion of technique ensnares us, and the texture of our personalities is affected. The American *image* is couched not in causes or events but in images picked up by constant involvement in vicarious activities. Thus, popular culture becomes part of a vast global treasure house or junkyard. Intimate electronic involvement of nations and races is changing presuppositions and perspectives. We are becoming part of the exterior activities everywhere.[3]

New mass media (especially television) have greatly increased the visibility of the entertainer and inflated his general importance. No movie star who has not been on television rates as high as even moderately successful television stars. The lines connecting hero, artist, and salesman have merged.[4]

The nineteenth-century robber baron grabbed off our natural resources and gorged himself during what V. L. Parrington calls the Great Barbecue. Business is business. Now show business is business. By their celebrities shall ye know and note them.

These advertising and public relations techniques have spilled over into politics, art, journalism, criticism, education. Image-making is revealed in everything we do, say, or see. The question is no longer "Do you like me?" but "Do you like my shadow?" As in Plato's allegorical cave, we have so mixed illusion and reality that our place in the world is determined by prestige. We mistake the shadows for ourselves, turning from the three-dimensional emancipator to the two-dimensional entertainer.

The popular imagination is plagued by extravagant expectations. We expect anything and everything. Masters of the entertainment industry work day and night to oblige: a television spectacular every week, a literary masterpiece every month, a new celebrity every season. The 1976 bicentennial was a national orgy of celebrities and celebration.

Celebrities are part of the American daydream, suspended between the long shadows of Rousseau and of Darwin. We are eternally drained by our allegiances to the natural man, on the one hand, and to the naturalistic man, on the other. Pioneer-believer at the same time we are pioneer-brute, we see every log cabin as a potential Shangri-la, knowing that the land is dark and bloody ground. We want both at the same time. The double want can never be satisfied and turns out to be a lasting crucifixion. The nails that bite the flesh from the outside turn out to be inside. Self-destruction is self-generated.

One of the earliest activities from which the celebrity came was spectator sports. Sports are a separate physical culture of our time. The obsession of the common man, sports are something he can observe, talk about authoritatively, cast in old heroic patterns. He can immerse himself emotionally and viscerally in sports, finding a sense of identity and destiny. Sports engage the time, energy, and money of the people to a far greater degree than science or the humanities, giving form and substance to much in American life. Hence the 1981 baseball strike was a national disaster.

Little wonder that baseball produced Babe Ruth. His monument is Yankee Stadium, the House that Ruth Built. George (Babe) Ruth came from a Baltimore charity school. After his first Homeric swat, on May 6, 1915, he continued to break records in a game designed for statisticians as well as spectators. In 1919, Ruth hit the longest home run then recorded. In the 1926 World Series, he pointed to a distant spot and yelled at the hooting fans, "I'll knock it out there for you!" He did. Out of such episodes come celebrities.

After that, legend takes over. Cultivating a Bunyanlike stance and appetite, Ruth ate eleven hot dogs in one afternoon. He also liked stiff drinks. Referring to Ruth's weakness for alcohol, teammate Lefty Gomez said: "He's the only man in the United

States that if you took a pint of blood, it would need a revenue stamp.''

Other stories featured the Babe giving sick children special attention and a paralyzed boy raising himself in the excitement of seeing him hit a home run. Psychotechnical tests proved that Ruth's eyes functioned twelve times faster than average. They also demonstrated that he outdid 499 out of 500 men in the responsiveness of his nerves. He was the Sultan of Swat; Beowulf at bat; a wonderworker who hit three World Series home runs in one afternoon. "God was with me," he said, "or I couldn't have done it."

A stream of celebrities has performed on America's fields, courts, and gridirons since Babe Ruth's day. He remains the pattern maker in sports, even though Hank Aaron eventually hit more home runs. Sitting in the bleachers as new aspirants go to the plate, munching on our Baby Ruth candy bars, we remember him still.

The boom in other professional sports (especially football, basketball, and hockey) has created a variety of celebrities. Not only players but sports come and go—such changes are complicated. We know little about the changing audience, the evolving aesthetic, the heroic climate. In the early 1970s conventional wisdom held that professional baseball was on the way out. The action was too slow, the strategy too cerebral for television audiences. But in the late 1970s, baseball made a dramatic comeback; interest in basketball began to wane. Out of nowhere, a tennis fad developed, and with it, a whole new set of celebrities, male and female. There is no explaining taste, fads, or celebrities.

The most ephemeral field, by everyone's admission, is popular music. Rock groups are hardly in before they are out. As a group ritual, the rock concert persists, but the faces of those staging it change constantly.[5]

"It is unlikely that any major trend is going to overtake us," *Billboard* (the industry's chief trade journal) predicted in 1975. Wrong. Suddenly, disco burst on the scene, by 1977 virtually owning *Billboard's* record charts. *Saturday Night Fever*, released in December 1977, made the prize-winning statement about the new rage:

> With a racially and ethnically-integrated cast and musical soundtrack as a backdrop, the hero and heroine (John Travolta and Karen Lynn Gorney) meet, dance, pair off, dance, flirt, dance—all on the urban disco floor. . . .[6]

Soon disco was the dominant background music on television programs and commercials and on movie soundtracks. An estimated 10,000 new dance halls opened, with spotlights, flashing colors, costumes, high-volume music, and special effects (such as laser beams and fog machines). Had we finally found a dance form in which everyone could play celebrity?

On the side lines, fans of former celebrities recalled how fickle is Dame Fortune. Take the case of the king himself, Elvis Presley. His 250 million records and thirty-one movies seemed to guarantee him a life-long adulation. As it turned out, life was not to be long. At forty-two Presley was dead, apparently of a drug overdose, and a host of imitators scrambled to fill his shoes.

Things even began to fall apart for Hugh Hefner, the publicist and Bunnymaster who had become a genuine publisher-celebrity as creator of *Playboy*. Graduating from high school in 1944, serving in the army, working for *Esquire* as a promotion copywriter, Hefner was making fifty dollars a week in 1951. Refusing a raise, he quit, put out the first issue of *Playboy* on a bridge table in his kitchen, and began a reign of notoriety that has lasted two decades.

In Russia, the leading satirical magazine, *Krokodil*, took a more elevated line. They praised *Playboy* because Hefner's imagination was indeed inexhaustible. Meanwhile, Italy, Germany, and France arranged for their own foreign editions of *Playboy*, edited and printed in Milan, Paris, and Munich. By 1970, a typical holiday issue of *Playboy* had 350 pages. In America, more money was spent buying it at newsstands than had ever been spent during a thirty-day period for any event in the field of paid entertainment.

Spider-Man, introduced by his creator, Stan Lee, in Marvel

Comic's *Amazing Fantasy* in 1962, was the leading comic celebrity a decade later. The Hulk, Captain America, Superman, Captain Marvel, and Wonder Woman all had their followers, but Spider-Man was something different. He was a superhero in the Liberal Tradition, fighting drug abuse and pushers, organized crime, pollution, and bigotry. Like the McGuffey *Readers* of earlier times, he has helped to educate the young and to bolster up their patriotism. By 1975, both the country and Spider-Man had grown a bit weary of crusades and crusaders; perhaps that will change in the 1980s, if crusading returns to style. In any case, the decade will produce new larger-than-life figures in movies, on television, and in comic books. And they will have a common denominator: all will be celebrities.

NOTES

1. Gary Willis, "The Making of Yippie Culture," *Esquire*, November 1969, p. 135.

2. Pamela Ecker, "My Affair with Farrah," in *Popular Culture Reader* (Bowling Green, Ohio: Popular Press, 1978), pp. 210-16. See also James Monaco, *Celebrity: The Media as Image-Maker* (New York: Dell Publishing Company, 1978).

3. See Walter Ong, *The Barbarian Within* (New York: Macmillan, 1964).

4. Patrick Hazard discusses these matters in "The Entertainer as Hero," *Journalism Quarterly* 39 (Spring 1962).

5. See Bill Owens, *Our Kind of People: American Groups and Rituals* (Livermore, Calif.: Working Press, 1975).

6. James von Schilling, "Disco-mmunity, or I'm OK, You're OK, America's OK, So Let's Dance," in *Popular Culture Reader*, p. 260.

FURTHER READING

Bruno, Michael. *Venus in Hollywood* (New York: Stuart, 1970).

Campbell, Joseph. *The Hero With a Thousand Faces* (New York: Meridian Books, 1949).

Fishwick, Marshall. *The Hero: American Style* (New York: Van Rees Press, 1969).

Greene, Theodore. *America's Heroes: The Changing Models of Success in American Magazines* (New York: Putnam's, 1972).

Klapp, Orrin E. "Hero Worship in America," *American Sociological Review* 14 (February 1949), pp. 53-62.

Monaco, James. *Celebrity: The Media as Image Makers* (New York: Dell Publishing Company, 1978).

Nocera, Joseph. "Tom Wolfe at the Keyboard," *Washington Monthly* (March 1980), pp. 20-26.

Wecter, Dixon. *The Hero in America* (New York: Charles Scribner's Sons, 1941).

9
SUPER STAR

I beheld Satan as lightning fall from heaven.

St. Luke

Almost everything that could go wrong for America in the 1970s did. Vietnam set the tone abroad, Watergate at home. Inflation rose, the dollar fell, and gas gave out at the pumps. One of the few bright spots was the bicentennial. For a brief bright moment, as the nation reached 200 years, all was well. We had made it!

At year's end, a rejuvenated Hollywood checked box-office figures. Who had dominated the screen during this year of historic nostalgia? The Pilgrim Fathers? Washington, Jefferson, Adams? Guess again—you may be surprised at the answer supplied by the *New York Times* on December 30, 1976:

> He's the biggest thing at the box office, no matter what you call
> him: Satan, Devil, Lucifer, Evil One, Hornie, Nick, Scratch,
> Mephisto. Not since *Rosemary's Baby* and *The Exorcist* has satano-
> phany paid off so well as now.

Traditional Man, steeped in common culture, would not have
been surprised at this. Nor should any student of common culture be. Satan has for centuries made every party, covered every
bet, dominated every medium. He turns up at the damnedest
times and places; no guest list is complete without him. He has
no rival as all-time Super Star.

Satan is eternal.[1] Like the Lord of Heaven Himself, Satan
represents a desire for unity, a bringing together of one being out
of many. Like Yahweh, he has a place in the rise of monotheism.
Both stand at the point where traditions and myths merge. Their
origins are shrouded in mystery. Satan is the incarnation of
physical and moral evil. Good is recognized by its contrast to
evil.

The New Testament is filled with satanic allusions. He is the
Adversary and Tempter of Jesus as well as of the people and
disciples around him. He appears as the evil one, the prince of
this world, the great dragon, the old serpent, the prince of the
power of the air, the antichrist. Christ speaks of a hell where the
fire shall never be quenched, where the worm dieth not, and is
himself tempted by a being whom he represents as sowing
weeds among the wheat. Jesus begins a rebuke to Peter, the rock
on which his church was to be built, with the words, "Get thee
behind me, Satan." When his enemies wished to discredit him,
they accused Jesus of being in league with the evil one, com-
plaining that by the prince of the devils casts he out the devils.
The contrast and contest between the radiant Savior and the
gloomy Adversary provide dramatic tension to the Gospels.

The resurrection—the central event of the Christian faith—
was directly related to this contest. By his death, Christ freed
men from death: the Gates of Hell could not prevail against
him. Christ's resurrection broke Satan's dominion. And yet
never was Satan so much talked about, so feared, as after
Christ's victory and the completion of his redemptive work.

Paul wrestles constantly with the problem of evil. He holds Satan responsible for the rise of the man of sin and for the mystery of lawlessness. The snares, the wiles, and the condemnation of the devil absorb him. St. Paul goes so far as to call Satan the god of this world. The Revelation of St. John contains the most graphic and imaginative demonology of the New Testament. We confront a beast whose number is six hundred and three score and six—which, according to John's mystical symbolism, means Nero. The Roman emperor who opposed Christianity so savagely becomes an incarnation of Satan. But the city that reigns over the kings of the earth (Rome) shall fall. So will Satan, who comes to deceive the four corners of the earth, Gog and Magog, to gather them together in war. He has not fallen yet.

The Personality of Evil saturated early Christian thinking. Satan attained full stature with the development of Christian doctrine. Demons, fallen angels who yielded to the fascination of women, fascinated St. Justin the Martyr. St. Cyprian called women instruments by which souls were possessed. Tertullian was even blunter: he called females the gate of hell.

Origen taught that Satan possessed free will and the power to choose between good and evil. Position in the ranks of evil creatures, he said, was determined not by essential nature but by progress in wickedness. In the centuries after Origen's death, a familiar image of Satan developed, along with another popular name (devil, from the Greek *diabolos*). He was a disfigured angel with horns, batlike wings, and claws. But he could and did take on many other aspects.

In the popular mind, the devil has long been associated with excesses, especially sexual. He is a master of orgies and has staged them for all manner of men and women. Henry III, bishop of Liege, was known to have sixty-five illegitimate children as a result of his extraecclesiastical binges. Few were as bold as Archembald, however, the tenth-century bishop of Sens. Taking a fancy to the Abbey of St. Peter, he drove out the monks, installed a harem of concubines in the refectory, and quartered his hounds and hawks in the cloister. Medieval Europe was swept by a terrific outburst of incubi and succubi. These were nocturnal visitors connected in Christian minds with devilry who indulged in liberties with the afflicted person, Burgo Partridge explains in his *History of Orgies*. They were particularly common in nunneries and seemed also to be highly infectious.

No less a writer than Petrarch gave the details of life in papal Avignon—a city filled with every kind of confusion, containing everything that had ever existed or been imagined by a disordered mind. It out-Babyloned Babylon. Nor were things always quiet in the older papal seat, Rome. Pope John XII was tried for sacrilege, murder, adultery, and incest. Balthasar Coass, who later served as pope, was deposed after confessing to notorious incest, adultery, defilement, homicide, and atheism. This is the same man who, while serving as chamberlain to Boniface IX, had kept his brother's wife as a concubine. These stories are not typical, but they are documented.

The flagellomaniac cult flourished throughout Europe. Day- and night-long processions of people headed by priests carrying crosses and banners walked in double file, reciting prayers and drawing blood from their bodies with leather thongs. Although Clement VI issued a 1349 bull against the heresy involved in self-flagellation, the practice continued and always soared during such calamities as earthquakes and plagues. In happier days, the May Games and the Feast of Fools provided unlimited orgiastic opportunities—as indeed *Faschuung* does in contemporary Germany.

Since historically accurate details of such events are rare, we are fortunate to have the 1445 indictment of the Feast of Fools prepared by the faculty of theology at the University of Paris. Priests and clerks cavorted about, it was alleged, dressed as women, panders, or minstrels. They mocked the mass, made indecent gestures, and recited scandalous verses. The devil was turned loose in holy places.

Nor could all this be excused or set aside as a fashion sanctioned by antiquity. On the contrary, the faculty claimed that what took place was due to original sin and the snares of devils. All such statements and warnings were ineffective. The feast continued far into the seventeenth century, when it was still replaced by secular festivals, like the election of an Abbot of Unreason or a Lord of Misrule.

Throughout the Middle Ages, the Church had to fight hard to keep out phallic saints (such as St. Fourtin) and to prevent the adoration of the Virgin Mary from becoming a fertility cult. Always the same discouraging tendency can be noted: to revert to the pagan and the ignoble, to make a mockery of the sublime. The tendency is always with us. Look at the names carved on the sides of churches and buildings, listen to the cruel laughter of children—their target an aging teacher who has devoted his life to educating the young. Observe people who have few responsibilities as they mimic and mock those who carry heavy burdens. Is there not more than a suggestion of the diabolic in all this?

There is no need to present a detailed history of orgiastic outbursts over the centuries (although this might add greatly to the sale of this book). That would be, so to speak, one damn thing after another. What we might do, before moving to other manifestations of Satan's power, is to note that the Age of Reason was irrationally fond of them. Eighteenth-century England was the home of the Hell-Fire Clubs, which specialized in satanic doings. But why not look, instead, at contemporary America? Satan Super Star has been doing extraordinarily well of late, and he has pinpointed the place where common culture, secret pleasure, and repressed drives meet: shall we take a peek at the game?

T. S. Eliot was mistaken. Ours is not a culture of a thousand lost golf balls, but of a thousand lost coitus. The game is sex. It begins in the gonads and—as the stand-up comics remind us—ends up not in heaven but in the law courts.

Or if popular novelists are right, in our neighbor's bedroom. Apparently, suburbia is full of nymphs and satyrs. "We're not trying to break out of our hedonism," a character in John Updike's *Couples* remarks. "We're trying to break into it." Sex is their joy, their glue, their fantasy, their narcotic, their hope, their revenge, their main form of communication. Harold Smith sleeps with Janet Appleby, and Marcia Smith with Frank Appleby; the crowd calls them the Applesmiths. Eddie Constantine and Irene Saltz bed down, as do Ben Saltz and Carol Constantine: they are the Saltines. So it goes.

What Became of Sin? was the intriguing title of a 1973 book by psychiatrist Karl Menninger. Gone with the wind. Today Eros is not merely respectable; he is a patron saint of popular culture. Writers, performers, artists adore him. Notice the lapel badges: if it moves, fondle it. Let's lock loins.

Instead of getting porn mail fourth class (pornography is a $2 billion-a-year industry), it now comes first class and personal. A recent piece invited me to purchase films showing physical love between naked men and women that goes *all out* . . . from oral stimulation to genital twitching!

"But I do all right now," a hesitant buyer was reported as musing. "How can these films help me?"

No matter how good you are, comes the voice from Outside, you can do better! New exciting techniques are constantly coming into circulation – from Europe, Africa, Asia, and young people in this country.

Paul Camus's comment in *The Fall* applies: "A single sentence will suffice for modern man: he fornicated and read the papers."

Modern man? Dare we assume it was really so different with our fathers or grandfathers? So musing, I glance at a 1907 photo. The man with a top hat, frock coat, and silver-headed cane is King Edward VII of England, Ireland, Scotland, Wales, and Dominions beyond the sea. The veiled lady beside him, languishing beneath the plush plumed hat, is Queen Alexandra. A frail parasol rests against her knee, a feather boa droops casually over her chair. And yet. . . .

While Edward was staring out at the world, the printing presses were turning out *Three Weeks* by Edward's subject Elinor Glyn. She created a mythical kingdom and a beautiful princess who was seduced and seduced and seduced—one time on a tiger-skin rug—enough to get Glyn to America to write movie scripts for Rudolph Valentino and to be interviewed by Mark Twain, who was impressed by the story of the couple that obeyed the natural demands of passion, and indeed kept on obeying them.

The process never *will* be fully described: Satan will see to that. Long after Edward VII and Miss Glyn had gone off to their reward (or punishment), the craving for witchcraft, satanism, and what one critic dubbed sexistentialism flourish. In its cover story for June 19, 1972, *Time* magazine documented "The Occult

Revival," reporting on witches' covens and devils' dens. Lucifer was, and has remained, hot property—a media Super Star. A leading rock group, the Rolling Stones, called themselves "Their Satanic Majesties" and proved it by driving some of their audiences into a murderous frenzy. William Peter Blatty's best-selling novel *The Exorcist* was turned into a movie that produced not only unprecedented profits but also mass hysteria. Newspapers reported a nationwide outbreak of demonic possession. The devil seemed to be replacing the cowboy as the standard box-office attraction.

If common culture comes, can Satan be far behind?

"Holy, holy, holy." Clitoris, fellatio, philanderers, polyandry, pornography. With themes like this to exploit, no wonder the devil has his due, and Satan is a Super Star. Would you like to hear the opening words for some of the most popular books and movies of the next generation? I'll be glad to tell you, but you have probably heard them before. The speaker was Eve and these were her words: "the serpent beguiled me, and I did eat."[2]

NOTES

1. In a more popular but profound way, C. S. Lewis explores the devil's strategy in *Screwtape Letters* (1939).

2. Among the best books on twentieth-century evil are Denis de Rougemont's *The Devil's Share* (1944) and Charles Journet's *The Meaning of Evil* (1963). Diabolic figures continue to dominate not only American films but also those of other nations—Japan, for example. The devil is having his due.

FURTHER READING

Bierce, Ambrose. *The Devil's Dictionary* (New York: Hill & Wang, 1957).

Blatty, William Peter. *The Exorcist* (New York: Harper & Row, 1971).

Carus, Paul. *The History of the Devil and the Idea of Evil* (London: G. Chapman, 1900).

Coulange, Louis. *The Life of the Devil* (New York: Knopf, 1930).

Journet, Charles. *The Meaning of Evil* (New York: P. J. Kennedy, 1963).

Langton, Edward. *Satan, A Portrait* (New York: Macmillan, 1945).

Lewis, C. S. *Screwtape Letters* (London: Windus, 1939).

10
PRINT CULTURE

Oh that my words were now written! Oh that
they were printed in a book!

The Book of Job

Words are the prime form of communication. No matter how
familiar we are with things, we master them only by verbalizing
them. What's in a name? Everything.

Written words are substitutes for sound—surface marks until
converted to sound again, either by imaging or by vocalizing.
Words are sounds that have certain meanings. In the words of
an anonymous eighth-century Chinese poet:

That art is best which to the soul's range gives no bound
Something beyond the form, beyond the sound. . . .

Words, Ralph Waldo Emerson wrote in his essay on *Nature*, "are signs of natural facts."

For millions of years, words were spoken: the oral-aural culture. Then came script, made possible by the alphabet and greatly enhanced by alphabetic movable type. Now words can be transmitted by radio waves and electricity, at 186,000 miles per second. Now words that once had only the vertical dimension of time have the horizontal dimension of space.

Words on the radio and television vanish into thin air: those in newspapers and books endure. Print is the medium of history. What would the historian or bureaucrat do or be without it? Radio may be our ears and television our eyes, but print is still our memory.

No one can give us all the news that's fit to print, but what is fitted to print today is what will be preserved and reread for years to come. The library is the collective mind of the civilization.

Print power is overwhelming. The invention of the printing press, a landmark in Western civilization, was the beginning of mass production. How would this book get to you if it were not printed?

The Print Era started long before Gutenberg's famous invention in the mid-fifteenth century. Print began slowly over 5,000 years ago with the development of pictographic, ideographic, and hieroglyphic symbols. Then came phonetic writing and the formation of alphabets. Gradually, man's intellectual processes and social organizations adjusted, and new modes prevailed. The influence of early books on the Renaissance, Scientific Revolution, and Reformation is incalculable; the word "bible" originally meant book. Print encouraged linear thinking, capitalism, communism, nationalism, and individualism. What we are is what we print and what we read.[1] Books are our communal memory and nourishment for our soul. They break the shackles of time. What we call civilization is built on literacy, which is a uniform processing of a culture extended in time and space by an alphabet.

If the modern world was called into being by the printing press, the key invention in the history of world media was the modern newspaper. Not only the content of news, but also of advertising, entertainment, and public perception was shaped and influenced by newspapers. While the earliest came from Europe, the United States was the first nation to separate the press from the official machinery of government. The nineteenth-century American press seemed to outsiders one of the great wonders of the world. In 1835, the Frenchman Alexis de Tocqueville noted:

> In the United States printers need no licenses and newspapers no registration. The number of periodicals surpasses all belief. Among the 12,000,000 people, there is not *one single person* who has dared to suggest restricting the freedom of the press.[2]

John Tebbel's *The Media in America* (1974) traces the role of newspapers in the founding of our nation and their continual development since. Freedom of the press, guaranteed by the First Amendment to our Constitution, has withstood attacks from governments, financial forces, advertisers, pressure groups, trade unions, corporations, and even the newspaper industry itself. The heroic action and courage of newspapers in the 1970s, when Watergate threatened to engulf the Republic, stand in a long line of battles. Despite the recent decline in the number of newspapers, their importance at all levels of society remains high. They are, Edward Whetmore points out, our culture bath. We bathe in massive amounts of information—not only news, but also special interests, sports, editorial, family, business—even visual humor, through cartoons and comics.[3] *Editor and Publisher* reported for 1980 that there were 1,750 daily newspapers and 8,000 nondailies published in the United States. About 60 percent of the dailies were owned by large chains.

In the 1960s a New Journalism surfaced, emphasizing the subjective and getting inside the story or event. Writers turned their backs on the rational and objective reporting that had become standard over the years.

These journalists report on the deaths of old myths. Tom Wolfe is a Daniel Boone who shows us the Las Vegas frontier. The real battles are no longer being fought along the Colorado or the Snake rivers, but along the Potomac and the Hudson.

Reporters like Woodward and Bernstein, whose work on the *Washington Post* exposed Watergate, have assured us that the newspaper is still a major bastion of our democracy.

In this short summary, I shall center attention not on newspapers but on magazines. They not only mirror today's culture in a unique way, but also seem to be assuming a larger and more vital role in the final decades of the twentieth century. While several of the most influential died in the 1960s (*Saturday Evening Post, Colliers, American*), the 1970s saw a renaissance with five new magazines appearing for every one that died. To sketch the main themes in the history of American magazines throws new light on the emerging common culture.[4]

Magazines published in colonial times tended to be by and for gentlemen. There were no illustrations, advertisements, or graphics. The tone was Olympian. "To preserve from oblivion those who have been useful to society is our goal," wrote the editor of *Monthly Anthology*. The usual subject was patriot, gentleman, and scholar.

The quickening pace of the nineteenth century and the democratic revolution of Jefferson and Jackson changed this. Magazines moved from the club to the marketplace. Aggressive capitalists carved out successful careers with popular magazines. Frank A. Munsey, S. S. McClure, and John B. Walker founded magazines that were their own, not connected with or limited to the traditions of established publishing houses. They pushed into the magazine business when they saw that conditions made it profitable. The popular hero of their era was Napoleon. "Millions still bow down to him," *Cosmopolitan* pointed out in 1908, "because he was the greatest embodiment of physical force in all ages."

A decade later, the Idols of Justice came into their own—politicians, clergymen, and bureaucrats engaged in social action. Teddy Roosevelt's image replaced Napoleon's. With the coming of World War I and America's entry onto the world scene, the hero became a manager of massive organizations—and was so portrayed in magazines. The task was to make an organizational society work at home while keeping the world safe for democracy abroad. Later generations would seek ways to reconcile individual independence with the structures of a rapidly changing society.

I. F. Stone, the founding father of underground publications, began publishing his irreverent *I. F. Stone's Weekly* in 1953. Radical in viewpoint but conservative in format, the *Weekly* tried to provide fact and opinion not available elsewhere. In 1955, the *Village Voice* appeared as a weekly, edited by Dan Wolf and published by Ed Fancher. Soon M. S. Aroni's *Minority of One*, Lyle Stuart's *The Independent*, and Victor Navasky's *Monocle* joined the movement. The most notorious addition was the *Realist*, started in 1958 by Paul Krassner, former comedian and sexual prophet-satirist. Proclaimed as the Magazine of Irreverence, Applied Paranoia, Criminal Negligence, and Egghead Junkies, it abounded in witty writing. The *Realist* was described by one writer as the *Village Voice* with its fly open.

With new writers and audience, journalism, and technology, the underground movement rejected the sterile old mythology and tried to create one based on political, sexual, and psychedelic realities. Read the *Berkeley Barb*, *Rolling Stone*, *East Village Other*, *Seed*, *Avatar*, or *Free Press*, and see how extensive the revolution actually was. That print could make so impressive a showing in what was supposed to be the Age of Visual Media showed how wrong Marshall McLuhan had been when he predicted its demise.

How many magazines were functioning in 1980? That figure depends on how one defines *magazine* and on what functioning is measured. Some surveys put the total figure as high as 20,000, which, in round numbers, includes about 10,000 industrial periodicals, called house organs or company magazines. They are ignored by the entrepreneurs in the business because they do not accept advertising and are given to readers, who are employees, customers, dealers, or prospects. There are 2,500 business magazines, commercially published periodicals catering to business and ranging from *Fortune*, published by Time, Inc., to the highly specialized *Roads and Streets*, issued by the Reuben H. Donnelley Corp., which has seventeen others. It also includes 400 published by associations.

To these publications can be added about 1,500 that deal with religion, 300 with education at different levels, 200 with labor. The remaining thousands are devoted to science, specialized sports, the arts, and various juvenilia.

What is the future of these magazines? Despite problems (especially financial) most authorities are optimistic. The enterprise is sound as long as printed communication is vital and has not been replaced by electronic means of communication. It is a highly segmented and diversified industry. Few generalizations can be made about its impact as a whole. The effects of the various types of periodicals both at home and abroad are easier to point out. One could go to almost any newsstands in the world and find not only American magazines but also imitators of *Time—The Link* in India, *Elseviers* in the Netherlands, *Tiempo* in Mexico, *Der Spiegel* in Germany, and *L'Express* in France.

Social effect has to do with the discharge of or a failure to discharge social responsibilities. The magazine press shares these responsibilities with all communications media, print or electronic, including the obligation, in a political democracy such as the United States, to provide the people with a fair presentation of facts, with honestly held opinions, and with truthful advertising. All but the subsidized periodicals hold to these goals within a certain framework, that of the business order, private initiative, profit making, and national interest. In the final analysis, the mass media support the system; they are part of our popular patriotism.

As business institutions, commercial magazines, consumer and specialized alike, have influenced the business world by stimulating the desire for products and services. This result has affected the living standards of readers, influencing their decisions about how they dress, eat, and use their spare time. The enormous consumption of cosmetics by Americans girls and women is in part due to the years of advertising in magazines. The sale of cars is heavily influenced by the advertising and special editorial content about new models.

The Magazine Advertising Bureau (MAB) has put forth the official concept of the influence of the general magazines. According to the MAB, the shaping of public opinion is first among general effects. The national magazine does not have the spot news function of either the newspaper or the radio. But being edited with deliberation, MAB said, it is read with equal deliberation and therefore has the unique ability to form a *mature* public opinion, nationally. It also is a reflector of American life, or what the owners think is American life. Life is not the daily headlines of the newspaper, nor is it the artificial dramatics produced by radio. The solid values of millions of American families are reported by the national magazine, unsensationally but vividly and accurately, in articles, fiction, pictures, and illustrations. The magazine is read more persistently than any other medium and is less perishable. It provokes results and receives reactions. Much magazine material later goes into books and motion pictures; reprints are made. The ripple effect is enormous.

Since the first modest ones came out in 1741, a number of factors have contributed to the continual changes (in format, appearance, and content) of American magazines, including improved technology, rising literacy and educational standards, and more sophisticated audiences. Both world wars enlarged the scope and concern of the American people, who had previously been isolated from much of the world by oceans. Since magazines were the favorite (sometimes the only) reading of millions of men and women in the armed services during World War II, they changed reading habits and thinking on a global scale.

Directly or indirectly, almost the entire population (including those who cannot read) is affected by magazines, which are a vital channel for communication.

As far as tomorrow's magazines are concerned, several trends are clear. The move toward specialized publications is overwhelming. "Whether you are a New Yorker, a pornographer, a skin diver, or a raiser of Nubian goats," publisher William I. Nichols wrote in the November 15, 1969 issue of *This Week*, "somewhere there is a specialty magazine made just for you." Every year Nichols' comment is confirmed further. As the number of magazines grows, so do the conglomerates. Multiple publishers like Dell, Fawcett, Hearst, Johnson, McGraw-Hill, Marvel Comic, William & Wilkins, and Ziff-Davis become ever more important. In 1980, McGraw-Hill was publishing forty-eight magazines plus three daily construction newspapers—to say nothing of scores of trade and technical books. This required over 800 full-time staff writers, 4,000 correspondents, and 2 news bureaus.

Since over 80 percent of the circulation of major magazines goes through the mails, magazines not only depend heavily on the postal service, but have also profited by preferential rates over the years. There was industry-wide consternation, therefore, when mailing rates soared in the 1970s. New laws said that magazines must pay their own way, upending delicate cost factors. In an industry where the average magazine represented only 0.6 percent profit per copy, what might this eventually mean?

Optimists are quick to point out that for every magazine that went under during the 1970s five new ones appeared. That growth rate would be envied by any industry. Will this continue in the problem-ridden 1980s?

Some claim that new technology will once again bring salvation. Can print advertising hold up against television? How will habits alter in the Electronic Age? What role will be played by photo-and-sound activated composition, electrochemical printing, facsimile transmission by satellite, and intermedia production? Have we not already seen the old magazine format adapted for television news and documentaries—especially in such programs as ABC's *20/20* and CBS's *60 Minutes*? Might not radio magazines emerge, first in underground FM stations, modeled on either KMPX or KSAN in San Francisco? Will technology soon allow us to order our *own* magazines, computerized for our individual tastes and available in our own living rooms?

The only limitation is the craving and creativity of the human spirit.

NOTES

1. Of the books that deal with print's profound influence, two have been particularly helpful to me: Harold Innis' *The Bias of Communication* (Toronto: University of Toronto Press, 1951) and Marshall McLuhan's *Understanding Media* (New York: Signet Books, 1964).

2. Jeremy Tunstall, *The Media Are American* (London: Constable, 1978), p. 24.

3. Edward Whetmore, *Mediamerica* (Belmont, Calif., Wadsworth, 1979), p. 32.

4. The standard reference is Frank Luther Mott, *A History of American Magazines*, 5 vols. (Cambridge, Mass.: Harvard University Press, 1930-68). Vol. 1, 1741-1850; Vol. 2, 1850-65; Vol. 3, 1865-85; Vol. 4, 1885-1905; Vol. 5, 1885-1905. For supplementary reading, see Theodore Peterson's *Magazines in the Twentieth Century* (Urbana: University of Illinois Press, 1972), and James L. C. Ford, *Magazines for Millions: The Story of Specialized Publications* (Carbondale: University of Southern Illinois Press, 1969).

FURTHER READING

Downs, Robert B. *Books That Changed the World* (New York: Mentor, 1956).

Lehmann-Haupt, Hellmut. *The Book in America: A History of the Making and Selling of Books* (New York: Bowker, 1951).

McLuhan, Marshall. *The Gutenberg Galaxy* (New York: Bantam, 1962).

Mott, Frank Luther. *Golden Multitudes: The Story of Best Sellers in the United States* (New York: Macmillan, 1947).

Sperling, Susan K. *Poplollies and Bellibones: A Celebration of Lost Words* (New York: Penguin, 1979).

Waples, Douglas; Berelson, Bernard; and Bradshaw, F. R. *What Reading Does to People* (Chicago: University of Chicago Press, 1940).

Wheeler, Thomas C. *The Great American Writing Block: Causes and Cures of the New Illiteracy*. (New York: Penguin, 1979).

11
ART CULTURE

But the Devil whoops, as he whooped of old:
"It's clever, but is it art?"

Rudyard Kipling

This much seems certain: nothing begins as art. People start out
to create *something*: a chair, vase, painting, palace. In all societies
the artistic impulse expresses itself according to traditional
needs and standards. The channel through which individual
effort flows is sanctioned form. Art, like every human activity,
mirrors the people and places of origin. Of course art is an
essential part of common culture.

In the twentieth century the gap between the artist and citizen has widened to a chasm. Despite an increased prosperity

that saw the rise of major museums, the popular press, art books, and films, the sense of alienation and outrage associated with movements like Fauvism, Cubism, Futurism, and Expressionism spread with every new exhibit. In 1916 a major art movement appeared under the label Dada—children's gibberish for hobbyhorse. Such art, the public was told, could only be experienced through complete devotion to the unconscious.

By now we can see that artists and writers were undertaking a major house-wrecking activity. They believed they had to clear out the debris of the past before art could move forward . . . an exciting and heroic proposition. But when and how could such art relate to common culture and the great tradition?

Art criticism became, and has remained, as mystifying as the art and movements it illuminates. In what sense, for example, have painters given us a polyphonic vision that parallels the music of Erik Satie or Arnold Schönberg? How can the idea of sharps and flats, usually applied to music, be used to explain modern fiction and poetry?

Other relationships have been explored and explained in such provocative works as those by the Spaniard Xavier Rubert de Ventos. In *El arte ensimismado* (Barcelona, 1963), he found strong parallels in forms of modern film, painting, and poetry that justified his theory of "Self-Absorption": each art is searching for its identity and trying to invent its own set of rules, avoiding anything that might make its message relative. A few years later (in *Teoria de la sensibilitat*), he declared "Self-Absorption" to be a special form of realism. The major task artists had set for themselves was not to *resemble reality* more closely, but rather *to be real*. The pertinent question changed from "What is art?" to "When is art?" That is, when, and under what circumstances, does a stone, a billboard, a soup can, or an advertisement carry both appearance and suggestion, presence and reference?

In the 1970s (especially in *La estetica y sus herejias*), systems theory arose to encompass the new fiction, Ludwig Wittgenstein's philosophy, the sociology of small groups, and the plastic arts. Realism, de Ventos decided, is a special case of an even more general phenomenon, which he calls puritanism. Today's artist has entered into a new bondage: revealing society to itself. He might reject the conditions of society, but he is not free to be indifferent to them. This theory is especially illuminating, as we shall see, when applied to America's Pop Art.

The link between technology and art is becoming very strong. The sculpture of David Smith drew on the methods and forms of industry and machine shops: he was primarily a welder. Art schools are beginning to teach electronics, wiring, and glass blowing. Not only oils and brushes, but transformers, laser rays, mercury vapor, and carbon filaments are part of the art world. Artists are using aluminum, polyesters, and motors to create art that beeps, buzzes, and pops.

The most radical change is the acceptance of accelerating change as the norm. After decades of holding back, the break-through for modern art in the popular mind has occurred. Even ads have popped. The studio has become a workshop where images are manufactured and new materials tested.

Paintings are no longer stories in pigment hung on museum walls but are raw hunks of reality, shouting out and insulting those who pass by. Distortion is as important as color; our world is as distorted as it is colorful, and art reflects that. Instead of recording existing conditions, arts condition themselves . . . wild, odd, structureless. In them, one finds no sense of toeing the line or of compromising. Moderation is the suburbia of the mind.

The movement was from words to images. "Don't tell us, show us! Don't speak the truth—be it!" Are we listening to a bearded painter addressing a Pub Club or a bearded messiah speaking to his disciples?

Abstract painting, which swept America after World War II, was a daring, vitalizing movement. Art became preoccupied with and answered only its own processes. A painting became a painting—nothing more. Seeing it became a sensual experience—nothing more. The act of painting, not the completed canvas, became the creative focus.

The move was from realism to reality. Painting no longer stopped with the brush. It dripped from paint cans, made tangled webs of lines and spots in a brisk junglelike pattern. Suggesting the dynamics of the Secular City of which theologians were writing, Action Painting was an apocalyptic vision of a culture living out nightmares. Jackson Pollock, Willem de Kooning, Jasper Johns, Mark Tobey, Mark Rothko, and Franz Kline made their private anger, pain, and frustration the subject matter. In so doing, they may have moved the art capital of the world from Paris to New York, but it left the man on the street baffled and unimpressed. Also unimpressed were some cultural and social critics, including Tom Wolfe. In *The Painted Word*, he advanced the notion that three critics, Clement Greenberg, Harold Rosenberg, and Leo Steinberg, invented the theory, jargon, and mystique that made abstract expressionism the toast of the art world, that it was in fact the most literary of schools since only those who understood the words could hope to understand the painting. By the year 2000, Wolfe went on to predict, when the great retrospective of the period from 1945-75 was featured, the seminal figures would not be seen as Pollock, de Kooning, and Johns, but instead Greenberg, Rosenberg, and Steinberg.

And what will that mid-twentieth-century era be known as? The Era of the Painted Word!

Whether or not they agreed with Wolfe's analysis, many painters tired of abstraction and turned to the everyday world for their subject matter and inspiration. It was a wild swing of the pendulum—polar opposites are companions in the art culture of our time. From contradiction and tension has come a new vitality that has affected every level of society.

By the mid-1960s, a flourishing new school was taking as its subject matter billboards, cars, giant hamburgers, ice cream cones, and soup cans. On the surface, the pop artists seemed to be mocking the Great Tradition. In retrospect, we see that they were attempting to preserve it.

What makes any tradition great is adaptability. Why should modern art stay inside a single mode or tradition, when such areas as physics, biology, politics, linguistics, and theology are exploding? Why should beauty, for instance, remain an absolute criterion for the visual arts? The French painter Jean Dubuffet suggested that the use of beautiful and ugly to describe objects was merely an outworn convention. His own work, he insisted, was an effort to rehabilitate scorned values.

Why, a new generation of artists asked, concentrate on wild flowers and tame damsels, or on squares and splotches? Why not look at comic strips, hot rods, toothpaste ads, billboards—consensus products of our extravagant, big-breasted, one-born-every-minute society? Why not try dayglow colors, benday dots, acrylics, and neon tubes?

Our fascination with realism and representational technique stretches back ten generations to colonial American painting. This trend continues unbroken right into the twentieth century, with artists like Charles Demuth, Georgia O'Keeffe, Stuart Davis, and Charles Sheeler. During the 1950s, a London coterie called the Independent Group studied cybernetics, soap operas, mass media, pop music, violence in films, and styles of autos. The group analyzed *Esquire, Mad,* and *Playboy;* observed and began to comment on our obsession with food, sex, and plumbing. American Studies crossed departmental lines and raised new questions to relate not only to art but also to life—and to act in the gap between the two. The natural setting for art was not in the museum but in the street. Nothing is outside the ken of art. By following this premise, pop artists Robert Rauschenberg, Larry Rivers, Jasper Johns, and Roy Lichtenstein were able to revive aspects of common culture that had been lost for generations. Their work made the case for renewal.

Their impact can only be understood against the rapid succession of art styles and schools in the United States. For generations, the fine arts had been subservient to Europe, controlled by coteries. Like polo, debutante balls, and yachting, art was for the better—that is, *richer*—people. Public collections were few and mediocre. The great private museums were controlled by private patrons—the real collectors were the Morgans, Fricks, Rockefellers, and Mellons. In their marble palaces, guards chatted with occasional visitors to break the quiet and monotony. Art in America was a hothouse plant.

Then came World War II. Many great European artists—Mondrian, Leger, Chagall, Gropius, Ernst, Zadkine, Masson, and Breton, among others—came to the New World and freedom.

Art, like the atomic bomb, exploded, and the fallout went everywhere. With unprecedented vitality, art took new frontiers in stride: the primitive, abstract, three-dimensional, calligraphic, surrealistic. Symbolic acts began to take on visual forms. Authentic intensity aroused admiration and imitation; overnight, the long-provincial United States was becoming central.

With undreamed of opportunities, models, and markets, native Americans joined the movement and began to shape it.[1] The most powerful of these was a Westerner who had studied with regional painter Thomas Hart Benton before moving East— Jackson Pollock (1912-56). Tall, rugged, partially bald, Pollock gave the impression that every word he spoke cost him something of his life. Covering huge canvases with glowing bands of color, Pollock created living energies in space, electrified his viewers.

If this was the crest of American art culture in the 1950s, what did it say about the position of the artists? What meaning (if any) could we attach to those flowing patterns and irrational explosions? Were the artists at war with the rational, mechanistic world in which they were living? Was it the ultimate snobbery of literary painting accessible only to the precious few who had the word? Was it in essence a put-on?

Marcel Duchamp, who had been art's *enfant terrible* a generation earlier, suggested a new concept called the aesthetics of impermanence. In the new electronic age, art objects are merely interludes, intervals in the life of the maker or viewer, temporary energy centers, glowing like a light bulb for a brief moment, then going out. Plays, concerts, paintings retire, leaving only the memory and image for those who were involved.

Such impermanence, Duchamp and his coterie insisted, was, in the contemporary world, both cultural *fact* and stylistic *device*. Those who did not know the grammar and language of the media could not hope to understand. This was the chief axiom of the new Artculture.

What about his own earlier work, one might ask Duchamp. Was it also the victim of the aesthetic of impermanence? Yes, he was quick to admit. His famous nude had descended the staircase for the last time. Her time had passed—but the influence of

Duchamp and his contemporaries would suface again, with pop art.

Pollock was the symbol of revolt against existing conventions in imagery, the leader in a common search for ways to contain a new vision. That vision was changing rapidly, all over the world —and New York captured it best. Characteristics were immediacy, spontaneity, encounter, abrasion, experimentation, and feeling. These have continued, no matter how much subject matter and angle-of-vision have changed. Pollock was killed in a sports car accident, going 120 miles per hour when his car left the road. He was forty-four.

From the first, pop art was international.[2] Indeed, the name itself seems to have been coined in London. The germinal figure, Claes Oldenberg, was born in Sweden but went to New York in the 1950s. The Big Apple was never brighter. Walking Manhattan's teeming streets, he tried to find outer form for what was found within himself. Favoring immediate, direct experience, Oldenberg turned out three-dimensional models of hamburgers, hot dogs, and birthday cakes. His technique was to isolate a mass-produced article from its normal surroundings, remove its functional value, substitute a different material from the original, and present it on an unexpectedly monumental scale. He hoped to open our eyes (as art has often done in the past) to aspects of experience generally considered outside the world of art, to literally reveal a new world. The movement represented the pendulum swinging away from abstract painting:

ABSTRACT	POP
supersubjective	superrealistic
view from inside	view from outside
art for art's sake	antiart
serious	playful
personal gesture	public trivia
the unusual	the commonplace

Pop was joined by op (optical), which set up color vibrations in such a way that after-images and apparent motions were stimulated. Most of these forms exploited such tricks by trial and error rather than by formula. It was an art of pure physical sensation, deliberately avoiding symbolic language, staying within the boundaries of the tangible objects of which it consisted. Impersonal, controlled, calculated, it sometimes created a kind of self-hypnosis, with special distortions that created a sense of moving depth.

Drawing from the vernacular in which popular forms had existed for decades, artists accepted the values of mass society and environment, seeking not the unique but the typical. Five artists were close enough in spirit and subject to form a school: Andy Warhol, Roy Lichtenstein, Claes Oldenburg, James Rosenquist, and Tommy Wesselman . . . the Super Realists.

Of the five, Andy Warhol was the most notorious and famous.[3] Open, flexible, accepting, he wanted to be like a machine. Instead, he became a celebrity but continued to live with his mother and to wear a tattered leather jacket. In addition to oil canvases (those of Campbell soup cans were the most famous), he made movies in a studio called The Factory. One of them, *The Chelsea Girls*, cost $1,500 and netted $1.5 million. In addition to stars named Viva, Ultra Violet, and Ingried Superstar, he hired a bit player named Valerie Solanos, who shot and seriously wounded Warhol in 1968. Recovering in the hospital, he dictated (without a change or correction) a novel called *A*, while Valerie organized *SCUM* (Society for Cutting Up Men).

Sculpture was also affected by the new movement and aesthetic. Junkyards became resource centers; ideas of beauty gave way to ideas of power. Favorite adjectives became strong, brutal, archetechtonic. David Smith was the favorite, but Barnett Newman, Anthony Smith, and Robert Grosvenor had many followers.

Variations were not only technical but regional. A vicious neo-Dada grew up in California, that land of doggie dinners, topless go-go girls, perfumed toilet paper, and fun cemeteries. Bruce Conner was a successful practitioner, depicting extermination camps, lunatic feminine adornment, and the carnage of Hiroshima. Funk tried to link jazz, sex, and revulsion, as the in definition suggested: "When a man gets orgasm from a prostitute, he has funked her. It shouldn't have happened."

Some thought pop art shouldn't have happened—but it did, and there was no turning back. Could the new art use newly sanctioned experiences and techniques in a way that would create valid artistic expression? Even those who thought the answer was yes admitted to a grave limitation. One of the truisms of communication is that the redundant is as boring as the absent. How many soup cans are enough soup cans? Boring boring boring.

In some instances, the movement became self-defeating. Musician John Cage began writing music that was made up of silences. Dancer Paul Taylor took as his motto "Down with choreography!" Can an art form self-destruct? What about content? And meaning?

By 1978, some perspective on the wild outbursts of the previous decades seemed possible. Robert E. Mueller wrote:

> Pop Art cracked the stalemate of abstract art and let flow many of the newer forms of art current today. It also allowed some of the older forms to reflower. Pop Art was realistic, and through its popularity realism came back full force.[4]

Questions about and comments on the Artculture of our times abound. Since art had been lost, why not Found art? Can we call art things collected from a garbage heap, then exhibited in a museum? Are *all* things art—or do they at least have the potential of becoming art? Can artists concern themselves with total ecology, working with fire and air, placing objects on the ocean floor, directing the flight of birds, signing the Grand Canyon? Does a painting recall the memory of a past experience or current event? Does it call upon our intellect or tap the unconscious subliminally?

Such questions could only be raised after the inroad of pop art. Life inside and outside the museums has been affected. When Mary Quant introduced miniskirts to London, they became part of an art-scene, complete with rock music, dead birds, thigh-high hunter's boots, and multimedia shows. As John Aldridge has noted, the rise of a unisex style was related to pop art; the democratization of the human body results in a new style . . . a corporate type of female beauty and male handsomeness.[5]

Even the Soviet Union, which has so vigorously opposed modernism, abstraction, and decadence in modern art, has been interested in American art culture. In 1976, Russia invited Jamie Wyeth and Larry Rivers to visit and lecture on painting. By then, an offshoot of pop art, photo-realism, was receiving wide attention. Such photo-realists as Robert Bechtle and Richard Estes were taking color photos and reproducing them precisely in paint on canvas with the help of a slide projector. Critics denounced this triumph of mediocrity and "visual soap opera." In 1973 Douglas Davis wrote an essay on "The Decline and Fall of Pop"—a movement that fell before many Americans knew of it. Davis argued that despite all the publicity, pop art had never really been popular. Strong on humor and irony, its mode of action was passive and accepting. The central flaw or weakness was an indifference to personality and individuality. Line after line of soup cans or cardboard boxes was, in the last analysis, merely boring.

By the mid-1970s, pop was fading. By the time Robert Hughes produced his television series on modern art for the BBC (turned immediately into a 1981 book called *The Shock of the New*), it was fashionable not only to pronounce pop art dead, but to tell why:

> It was a delusion. Pop art could not survive outside the museum, since contact with a message-crammed environment at once trivialized it.[6]

A consensus culture was forming, but pop art was outside it. Cultists and elitists will continue to buy, display, and explain both abstract and pop painting. But the mainstream will go back to the creative source. It always does.

NOTES

1. A full account is given by Dore Ashton, *The New York School: A Cultural Reckoning* (New York: Viking Press, 1972).

2. The best short summary is Christopher Finch's *Pop Art* (New York: Vista, 1968).

3. See G. R. Swenson, interview with Andy Warhol, *Art News*, November 1963.

4. Robert E. Mueller, "The Private Turning Public: The Visual Arts and Mass Communication," in Richard Budd and Brent Ruben, eds., *Beyond Media* (New York: Hayden, 1978), p. 281.

5. John Aldridge, *In the Country of the Young* (New York: Doubleday, 1970), p. xiv.

6. Robert Hughes, *The Shock of the New* (New York: Knopf, 1981), p. 354.

FURTHER READING

Ashton, Dore. *The New York School: A Cultural Reckoning* (New York: Viking Press, 1972).

Lenihan, John H. *Showdown: Confronting Modern America in the Western Film* (Champaign: University of Illinois Press, 1980).

Rubert de Ventos, Xavier. *Heresies of Modern Art* (New York: Columbia University Press, 1980).

Sontag, Susan. *Against Interpretation, and Other Essays* (New York: Farrar, Strauss, 1966).

Wolfe, Tom. *The Painted Word* (New York: Farrar, Strauss, and Giroux, 1975).

12
MACHINE CULTURE

By thud of machinery and shrill
steam-whistle undismay'd. . . .

Walt Whitman

Walt Whitman was not dismayed, but in the 1980s, many of his
countrymen were. Although we had moved from steam engine
to space, we were uneasy about our technology. Nuclear power
plants were potential perils to millions—to say nothing of nuclear bombs. Less spectacular, but increasingly ominous and
omnipresent, were industrial pollutants and wastes that caused
everything from ingrown toenails to cancer. The United States
was the most advanced element of Machine Culture. Yet the big
question was: Can we civilize the machine?[1]

Technology (from the Greek root *techne*, art or skill) is the physical backbone of the industrial world. The entertainment industry—one synonym for popular culture—depends on that technology and know-how. It is a series of events and techniques for duplicating and multiplying materials, sounds, and images.

Nothing has been duplicated and multiplied more than monsters—a point of departure for our chapter on machine culture. The offspring of Dracula, that blood-sucking vampire, have become legion; so have those of the Wolfman and the Hulk. King Kong haunts our national memory; he seems by now to *own* the top of the Empire State Building. Mary Shelley's vivid portrayal of Frankenstein has haunted us for over a century. William Morris's *News from Nowhere* (1890) described irate workers smashing machines to return to the "Good old days" of handicraft—a theme continued in Samuel Butler's *Erewhon*, W. H. Hudson's *A Crystal Age*, and E. M. Forster's *The Machine Stops*, all of which portray technology as a habit-forming drug.

No longer is it fashionable to shudder at every scientific advance and to note that we are just one step closer to George Orwell's *1984* or Aldous Huxley's *Brave New World*, where sex, sports, and soma prevail; and people chant:

> Orgy-porgy, Ford and fun
> Kiss the girls and make them One.
> Boys at one with girls at peace;
> Orgy-porgy gives release.

But do we want the kind of release found by a nine-year-old boy named Joey who wanted to be run by machines. He put together an elaborate life-support system composed of radio tubes, light bulbs, and a breathing apparatus. Joey ran imaginary wires from a wall-socket to his stomach, so he could digest his food. His bed was rigged with batteries, a loudspeaker, and monitors to keep him alive while he slept. Joey was living out his autistic fantasies in a machine culture.

Such alarming episodes have caused some to reject science and its enslavement, to hark back to Rousseau and the Noble Savage.[2]

But if these romantics break a leg, will they forego the hospital? Or the antibiotic for an infection? Or the jet plane in favor of the oxcart?

Technology is a branch of moral philosophy as well as science. Great thinkers of the past have not sought technological humans, but humanized technology. "If we continue to place God in the machine," Roger Burlingame warns in *Background of Power*," we shall be at the mercy not of the machine, but of its high priests who know better and are thus in a position to exploit our ignorance."

People want to turn to something, or somebody, who has the answers. For Traditional Man, that somebody was God; for Modern Man, science. He puts self above neighbor; state above church; and science above all.

Intrigued by new gadgets, drugs, metals, and short cuts that scientism (false science) provides, the public values applied science over basic science. And the results are appalling. Landscapes are strewn with outmoded eggbeaters, last year's neon signs, crinkled automobile fenders, empty beer cans.

Getting and spending, we lay waste not only our powers but also our happiness. *Things* are substitutes for pleasure. For Keats, a thing of beauty is a joy forever; we have shortened the line: a thing is a joy. If it threatens to last forever, we junk it for a shinier mode.

Science, having proclaimed God's power in the hands of humble men, has become itself a false messiah in the hands of greedy ones. It is the old Baal business all over again, chromeplated, jet-powered, gimmick-laden. The new commandment is plain: love things and use people. The reverse proposition, to love people and use things, was outmoded.

Scientism has opened a gap between science and ethics. Men have produced hydrogen bombs while admitting that no moral society would sanction their use. In their efforts to preserve humanity, they find themselves becoming less than human. Bombs keep coming. We have a job to do, their manufacturers say—as if they do not also have a responsibility.

Scientism has leaped out of the laboratory and into classrooms, living rooms, and churches. It is as attractive to Communists as it is to capitalists. An unending international atomic squabble is inevitable. Both blocs are primarily devoted to *things* to solve their problems and to impress their allies.

Our scientists have warned us. The pictures of Albert Einstein in tears before a congressional committee and of Robert Oppenheimer in disgrace may seem to future historians to be the most significant of the twentieth century. "What have your one to my people?"

Some of our most creative technological minds are striving to bring variety to chromobile tail fins and to make the refrigerator light come on half a second quicker when we open the door. Is it for this that Galileo and Descartes and Einstein labored? Science hesitates to answer. Scientism does not. The answer is on the wall, in the form of a rising line on a graph. One answer, at least, although the final answer may be quite different, in a place where new models are not nearly so relevant as old mistakes.

Meanwhile, new models flood the market. We buy the car of tomorrow, only to find out tomorrow that it is the car of yesterday. We dispatch it to the junk heap and return like Sisyphus to the foot of the hill (or loan office) to begin all over again. The mad dash goes on forever, and our chase has a beast in view.

Man against the beast—not only the beast within him, but the beast riding in the back of the police car, trained, ready to leap and (if necessary) to kill. Will today's police dog become as critical in maintaining human decency as the sheriff's horse was a century ago? Or will zebras learn to respect one another's stripes, be they black or white? Can we rebuild and retool in technopolis?

This question need not dismay us, any more than retooling for a new automotive age need terrify Detroit technicians. No one is asking or expecting us to give up our archetypes, our way of life. When car manufacturers move engines to the rear, cars still go forward. We may abandon the killer-tactics of the tiger and still survive and prosper in the complex new jungle.

America's technician mentality shapes not only her assembly lines and vending machines but also all aspects of her culture. Apply that mentality to painting and sculpture and pop art emerges. Technology creates it own sense of time: dynamism is built into the model. Change becomes an annual ritual, a confirmed habit, an absolute. Innovation is the rule. Styles hardly come in before they move out. Color me Culture Lag.

The technician mentality abandons traditional notions of myth. Transcendence cannot be put on a blueprint or flow chart. The power that technology puts into men's hand is matched only by lack of understanding as to its meaning. Students of technology and the history of science warn that throughout the society, attitudes and assumptions are outmoded and inadequate. In *Christians in a Technological Era*, Scott I. Paradise admits he cannot think of one first rate theological mind in America who has dedicated his life to studying the meaning of technology. Does this help to explain our lack of viable mythology? And the turn to the occult, irrational, and emotional by the children of technocrats?

The question points up a baffling paradox. Automation, computerization, nuclear fission, and rocketry should have made us free—but they have only tyrannized us to a degree unparalleled in history. Our ancestors thought we would by now have built the Brave New World. Instead, we seem bent on blowing it up.

We must touch new godheads. Think how mythology could be enriched by encompassing electronic ecology, which studies the interrelationship of organisms in the whole universe. Until recently, ecology was largely the bailiwick of biologists concentrating on plant environments. Now ecologists see total environment not only as physical and biotic but also as cultural and conceptual. Material from the traditional humanities, arts, social sciences is included. Only interdisciplinary efforts can focus on the holistic man, who is moving into an era of *total environment*. Confronted with that movement, mythmakers have three choices: change, adapt, or retreat into pedantic triviality.

Whatever its faults, technology does change and adapt; in fact, it enforces obsolescence on the very machines that pour out of its cornucopia. The operative words are *mass production* and *assembly line*. In the popular imagination, one man gave us these things: Henry Ford. His mass-produced automobile was perhaps the most revolutionary object of this century. He put us on wheels. Aldous Huxley suggested (in *Brave New World*) that we change calendar dates from AD to AF (After Ford).

In 1908, Ford's first Model T came from his factory; five years later, the assembly line was operating. The rugged Tin Lizzie, ugly but useful, won a unique place in American poplore and dozens of nicknames: Little Bo-Creep, Rolls Rough, Wanderer of the Waistland, Bouncing Betty, Little Shaker, Lizzie of the Valley, and Passion Pot. Lizzie Lore was definitely in the American idiom. "I'm from Texas, You Can't Steer Me," "Sugar, Here's Your Daddy," and "Pike's Peak, Here We Come" left no doubt as to national origins.

Jokesters told of the aristocrat who paid $15,000 for a Rolls Royce but kept a Ford in the trunk to pull it out of mud holes. Or they recalled a Ford worker who dropped his wrench on the assembly line and was twenty cars behind when he picked it up. Neither Jove nor Jehovah was more remarkable than Henry Ford, who turned tin into automobiles.

Had you heard that new Fords would be yellow so that they could be sold in bunches like bananas? That Ford was going to paper the sky with flivver planes? That Model Ts were being shipped in asbestos crates since they came off the line so fast they were still hot and smoking? That the next Ford would come with a can opener, so you could put doors wherever you wanted them?

In two decades, Ford produced 15,456,868 Model Ts in thirty assembly plants, selling them for as little as $265 each. He put us on wheels. America, quipped Will Rogers, was the only country on earth where a man could ride to the poorhouse. Common culture never found a more admirable technician than Ford—unless it was the one Ford himself admired so much that he actually captured his last breath, put it in a bottle, and preserved it in a museum. His idol was a young inventor named Thomas Edison, who in 1875 decided to experiment with a talking machine. He saw it as a way of supplementing the newly discovered telephone, which was available only to the affluent. If others could have a cheap unit to *record* messages, perhaps these messages could go to a central station for rebroadcast. The ingenious Edison used a metal cylinder with spiral grooves and a piece of tinfoil to wrap around the cylinder. On it, the first five words ever recorded were: "Mary had a little lamb."

By 1878, he had formed the Edison Speaking Phonograph company and had written in his notebook a list of ten ways in which his toy might benefit humanity:

1. Letter writing and all kinds of dictation without the aid of stenographer.
2. Phonographic books, which will speak to blind people without effort on their part.
3. The teaching of elocution.
4. Reproduction of music.
5. The "Family Record"—a register of sayings, reminiscences, etc., by members of a family in their own voices, and of the last words of dying persons.
6. Music-boxes and toys.
7. Clocks that should announce in articulate speech the time for going home, going to meals, etc.
8. The preservation of languages by exact reproduction of the manner of pronouncing.
9. Educational purposes, such as preserving the explanations made by a teacher, so that the pupil can refer to them at any moment, and spelling or other lessons placed upon the phonograph for convenience in committing to memory.
10. Connection with the telephone, so as to make that instrument an auxiliary in the transmission of permanent and invaluable records instead of being the recipient of momentary and fleeting communication.

By the end of World War I, there were over 200 manufacturers of phonographs; the list Edison had made was being turned into reality. A music form called jazz made popular music a gold mine; over 100 million records were sold in 1927.[3] But the *real* boom lay ahead, when rock and roll (a blend of country music with rhythm and blues) surfaced in the 1950s. The one person who is often called the "father of the form" is Cleveland deejay Alan Freed. He coined the term "rock and roll," joined the staff of WINS radio in New York, and introduced Bill Haley's "Rock around the Clock," the first rock-and-roll single to reach the top of the charts. Meanwhile a shrewd promotor, Sam Phillips, drove all over the South looking for "a white boy who can sing colored. . . ." He found him in 1954 and recorded the performer's first hit. His name was Elvis Presley.[4]

The growth of other new electric media was just as spectacular and revolutionary. While Edison was improving his phonograph, others were developing the radio. Young David Sarnoff decided in 1916 to make radio a household utility in the same sense as the piano or phonograph, and the corporation he headed (RCA) did just that. Wireless transmission of images spurred the growth of television. A landmark was President Franklin D. Roosevelt's televised opening of the 1939 World's Fair. The growth after World War II was incredible. The number of sets jumped from 7,000 in 1946 to around 172,000 in 1948 and to over 5 million in 1950. Even theologians were awed. "Radio is like the Old Testament," Bishop Fulton Sheen said in *The Electronic Christian*, "hearing wisdom without seeing. Television is like the New Testament—wisdom becomes flesh and dwells among us."

So, by then, did cyberculture, which has to do with controlling or monitoring machines—especially computers. Information is gathered at different points along the river of communication, stored at a central pilot post or machine, then distributed to different parts of the system on request.

In cyberculture, the machine begins to take over from man, to know more, remember more, react more quickly than can any human being. Already computers check our taxes, reserve our airline tickets and hotel rooms, handle our subscriptions, do our banking. What will happen when—?

Putting it in this terminology helps show the link with the past, with the Luddites, who went around destroying the new spinning jennies because they were replacing spinning wheels in nineteenth-century Britain. What will happen when—?

The chief argument of the antitechnologists is pro-Frankenstein. Technology is a beast, created by humans but now beyond human control: it will destroy us. Other leading arguments are:

1. Those who work with machines become machines.
2. Not the workers, but the technocrats, benefit from this. Recall Charlie Chaplin in *Modern Times*—the prototypical image.
3. Technology forces us to consume things we neither need nor want.
4. Technology is the enemy of all things natural; God made the country, man made the cities. The updated name of this old argument is, of course, ecology.
5. Using mass communication and mass advertising, technology creates mass man, glued to the boob tube, enslaved by a slavish pop culture.

In *The Existential Pleasures of Engineering*, Samuel C. Florman suggests that fear motivates the antitechnologist. In a world plagued by inflation, unemployment, riots, and labor unrest, the machine makes a convenient scapegoat. Things are changing in a way we do not understand; and what we do not understand we tend to fear.

It is easy to forget how recent in our culture is our resentment of science and technology. Our civilization is founded on these things, is rooted in their achievements. The whole atmosphere surrounding the settling and peopling of America was one of scientific and technological growth. This factor impressed other parts of the world so much that when the International Commission for a History of the Scientific and Cultural Development of Mankind put out their official volume 6, *The Twentieth Century*, in 1966, the text read:

> In the 20th century industrialism became the dominant, moulding force in the countries of its origin; it spread into new areas and it offered a goal to which much of the world might aspire.[5]

Now there are conflicting goals and strategies for achieving them. The essential power has somehow moved from those who *use* energy to those who *produce* it (especially oil). It was not

Iranian armed force, but oil, that held America hostage in the embassy crisis of 1979-81.

America still had the achievement of Edison—but what if Con Edison could no longer produce electricity? And who cared how many Fords were produced in Detroit if there was no gas for their tanks? There are no easy solutions: yearning for them is a form of self-deception. What we must do is not denounce our technology, but understand and control it.

Technology dramatically widens the range and impact of popular culture—makes things that were once available to the privileged few available to the masses. When Lawrence Olivier did *Richard III* on American television, for example, more people saw it that one night than had seen it on a stage since Shakespeare wrote it. Kenneth Clark, James Burke, Alistair Cooke, and Jacob Bronowski can supply information on civilization, technology, America, or the ascent of man—with on-site film—that is new even to those who have spent their lives studying the fields.

The increase of leisure time—available to all age groups—has had an unmeasured effect. We have become culture consumers. Old skills have been revived: ceramics, stained glass making, glass blowing. The line between elite and popular, professional and amateur is ever more difficult to distinguish. Art and technology are not always enemies; they can and often are allies.

Meanwhile, our overseas allies (especially Japan, Taiwan, and West Germany) were using the technology of the 1980s so successfully that they were driving American products off the market. Almost all our cameras, television sets, and other precision instruments were being imported. American highways were no longer filled with Fords and Chryslers (even massive subsidies could not revive that ailing corporation), but with Volkswagens and Toyotas. Today's common culture has become machine culture. If we solve the technical questions involved, can we handle the economic and moral ones? There is no more crucial question.

NOTES

1. An excellent summary of the dilemma appears in John F. Kasson's *Civilizing the Machine* (New York: Grossman, 1976) and the many books

by Lewis Mumford, such as *The Pentagon of Power* (New York: Harcourt Brace, 1969).

2. These matters are fully explored in Theodore Roszak's *The Making of a Counter Culture* (Garden City, N.Y.: Doubleday, 1969).

3. See Roland Gelatt, *The Fabulous Phonograph, 1877-1977* (New York: Macmillan, 1977).

4. Many details are given in Carl Belz's *The Story of Rock* (New York: Oxford, 1972), and H. Kandy Rhode's *The Gold of Rock and Roll, 1955-1967* (New York: Dell, 1970).

5. Caroline Ware et al., ed., *The Twentieth Century* (New York: Harper & Row, 1966), p. 75.

FURTHER READING

Ellul, Jacques. *The Technological Society* (New York: Knopf, 1964).

Mumford, Lewis. *The Myth of the Machine* (New York: Harcourt Brace, 1967).

Muller, Herbert J. *The Children of Frankenstein: A Primer of Modern Technology and Human Values* (Bloomington: University of Indiana Press, 1973).

Sheen, Fulton. *The Electronic Christian* (New York: Macmillan, 1979).

Ware, Caroline et. al. eds. *The Twentieth Century* (New York: Harper & Row, 1966).

13
SPORTS CULTURE

Anyone who will tear down sports will tear
down America. Sports and religion have made
America what it is today.

Woody Hayes

Man has always loved to stretch his legs and run: the Olympics
affirm that. Leg stretching, both male and female, has become a
political issue: President Carter's decision to boycott the 1980
Moscow Olympics and to punish Russia for invading Afghanistan
affirms that. To compete and exalt is part of the human condition. But with the new blending of human training and electronic reporting, sports moved to a different cultural realm.
Sports has taken on the trappings of religion.

This blending may be, from the perspective of popular culture, a marriage made in heaven. If so, the moment of consummation, for America, is the Super Bowl. Michael Real sees it as "Mythic Spectacle":

> The President of the United States telephones plays to coaches in the middle of the night; astronauts listen in orbit; cabinet members, top corporate executives, and celebrities vie for tickets to attend the game in person.[1]

In its first eight years, the Super Bowl surpassed the seventy-year-old baseball World Series and the one-hundred-year-old Kentucky Derby as America's number-one sports spectacle. Commercial time on television during the game was the most expensive of each year since 1970. I will not here dwell on the logistics or statistics of the game—that has been done many times. Instead, I shall concentrate on the overt and covert religious implications. Therein lies the real significance of our fast-exploding sports culture.

Begin by making the historic connection. Go back over fifteen centuries and recall these words from Christendom:

> "Welcome, happy morning!" age to age shall say.
> Fortunatus (530-609)

For centuries that happy morning, that Super Sunday, was Easter. For many Americans, it is now the day of the pro football championship. The drama has switched from empty tomb to full stadium. How did this take place, and what does it mean? Have spectator sports replaced religion, become a theology of popular culture?

The questions will offend some. How can we speak of theology —Queen of Heaven—in the same breath with popular culture— Slut of the Marketplace? Theology is intellectual, erudite, profound; popular culture is visceral, infantile, trivial. They have nothing in common.

Look again. Both deal with right and wrong, tears and laughter, life and death. The authors of a lofty ontology and a lowly soap

opera both depend on assumptions, most of which are unrecognized, let alone questioned. Thanks to centuries of study,
theologians are in a better position to classify, analyze, and
criticize than are popular culturists. Theologians hold many
more university chairs. Paul Tillich defined religion as the state
of being ultimately concerned. What about all those concerned
with sports?[2]

God is all around us; so is popular culture. This is His world.
He made it and called it good. In God's world today, people,
nations, and continents are wired for sound. To study current
manifestations requires a theology.

"Theology" seems to many removed from their lives and
needs, an ancient enterprise eclipsed by science and modernism, kept alive by scholars who speak to each other, about
issues that few can define or understand: escatology, teleology,
systematics, liturgics. Popular culture, on the other hand, fills
our lives but has no place in academe. Dismissed as mere
entertainment (or worse), it frequently is turned aside. NO ROOM
IN THE INN.

Back to the ball game. Or, more accurately, to the *liturgy*, from
the Latin *liturgia*, public worship, doing and saying things together. Music is frequently used, being one of the quickest
awakeners of the corporate conscience. (What is a football game
without a band?) Behind the electronic sound are ancient rites
and primordial dreams. No matter how much they have been
changed by commercialism (have not rites always lined someone's pockets?), they might be called religious (or at least sanc-
timonious). An Episcopal bishop recently commented that he
was tiring of the National Football League—it was too High
Church.

That hallowed game provides the basis not only for recreation
but also for religion. Our way of regarding religion as an *institu-
tion* might prevent us from seeing the "sacred" or sacrosanct in
everyday life.

We *want* religion locked into a pietistic Sunday morning service, and we mold our language accordingly. Look at the faces of
people listening to Easter sermons on the church's Super Sunday
(Easter), and compare them with the faces watching football's

Super Sunday. Where is there more involvement, angst, redemption?

Everyman (as John Bunyan called his Christian pilgrim) has become Everyfan. The metamorphosis is little studied or understood. Anyone can make qualitative judgments; little quantatative information is available. Even a stopwatch can provide new insights. There is surprisingly little action in television's "action-filled" bowl games. Pre and postgame activities consume 20 percent of the broadcast time; advertising another 15 percent; comments between play and halftime another 40 percent. Much of the remaining 25 percent "scoreboard clock time" goes for huddles, decisions, and penalties. In fact, during the four-hour telecast, the football is actually in motion for *less than ten minutes.*

What happens in those few minutes is traumatic. In Colorado (where the Denver Broncos roam), a fan attempted suicide by shooting himself in the head on the day after the Broncos fumbled seven times against the Chicago Bears. "I have been a Broncos fan since they got organized," he wrote in his suicide note. "I can't stand their fumbling any more."

He fumbled too—the bullet did not reach a vital spot. Otherwise, it would have been a splendid example of blood sacrifice demanded by a merciless God.

Traditional rituals were attuned to the seasons: throughout central North America, say anthropologists, they took the form of war games between tribes. How has this come down to our times? As "battles" between rival teams, with incantations, cheerleaders, and "fans" (short for *fanatic*) to urge helmeted warriors forward.

There are sacred songs, places (stadiums and bowls), pleas (Fight, team, fight!), special food (delivered to your seat by vendors), sides to sit on, colors to exhort (Go, big red!), an animal-object to pursue (pigskin), symbolic cloth (flags, banners) decorated with totems (eagles, pelicans, antlers). The champions of the two teams wear helmets over their heads—here also totems are painted. Incantations pour out. Pert priestesses leap into the air, throw arms out and legs back, excite the crowd to ecstasy. There are chants, cheers, songs. A chant is a phrase or group of phrases much repeated, often with claps and stomps. A cheer is a stanza, accompanied by rehearsed motions, with specific actions assigned to each word. A song has several verses, usually rhymed and set to music.

Our history of cheerleading is scanty, but generations ago, there were "yell masters" at colleges. No one knows when the secret language began:

> Boomilacka, boomilacka, boomilacka tee
> Rifraf refraf fifrac bee
> Ikidoo picky, wha hoo wha
> We got the big team RAH! RAH! RAH!

A well-cheered football game was played (Princeton vs. Rutgers) on November 6, 1869. The European tradition—individual comment or praise—was strong in America then but has given way to the collective. We *want* to be "part of the crowd." The art of collective cheering paralleled the rise of organized school sports. The "Princeton Locomotive" copied a chant that the New York 7th Regiment used moving south to fight the Rebels in the Civil War. Transformed to fit Princeton's needs, it became:

> Rah, rah, rah
> Tiger, tiger, tiger
> Sis, sis, sis
> Boom, boom, boom
> Aaaaaaaaaaaaaaaaaaaaaaah
> Prince-TON, Prince-TON, Prince-TON!

Countless imitations of simple chants with tripartite patterns flourish. Sometimes we know the author: D. A. Rollins Dartmouth cheer was introduced in 1878:

> Wah-hoo-WAH!
> Wah-hoo-WAH!
> Da-Da-Dartmouth
> Wah-hoo-WAH!
> Dart-MUTH, Dart-MUTH, Dart-MUTH!

Students at Yale got their Brekekekex, koax, koax, from the frog chorus in Aristophanes—and been croaking away ever since 1884.

Such things change with the times. African influence (real and imagined) was apparent in the 1960s, as in this California yell: "Uh Ungowa, Green and Gold Powa." A popular television ad, Kellogg's Tiger selling Sugar Frosted Flakes, can make an impact. A dozen yells feature Tiger's "Grrrrrreat."

What is at stake in a "friendly game" is a minutely observed and monitored battle between aggressive male teams that use cunning, deceit, and violence to attain their ends. Does this sound like a corporation or bureaucracy? Is the Super Bowl a mirror-image of Life Out There?

And what about Up There? Teams both play and pray to win. Some coaches insist on prayers in the locker room. The Miami Dolphins have a public pregame prayer. "How touching a scene," reports Colman McCarthy of the *Washington Post* for December 10, 1979. "Giant men, bruised and asweat, kneeling to acknowledge that however almighty their win may have been, there is still another Almighty, the Divine Coach. . . ." In such a scene, the true meaning of popular culture can be found.

First, we must concede that this *is* a religious experience, that we are witnessing not mere entertainment, but deep commitment.

Analyzing religious experience, Mircea Eliade posits two modes of thinking—sacred and profane. The sacralized life is filled with *mysterius tremendous*, shared by centuries of hunters and farmers for whom objects had not only function but also sacred dimension. Their cosmos was dominated by the power of *hierophony* (manifestation of sacred reality). A momentous thing happened: man was gradually de-sacralized, left with no sacred model outside the historic human condition. Doing away with hierophony encouraged pseudoreligion and secular mythology.

Writers who equate "sacred and profane" with "elite and popular" fail to see that there are sacred and profane elements in all levels of culture. Awed by the "sacred space" in Chartres, they fail to see such space not only in Versailles (where the architect designed a chapel so that only Louis XIV could see the altar) but also in Las Vegas and the Astrodome.

The sacred always goes bad unless working with the secular. The word becomes vaporous abstraction unless it becomes flesh. One falls into a dangerous trap by dismissing the modern world as trivial when much of it is de-sacralized. Things our rural forebears held sacred are no longer encountered or examined, but the idea of having sacred things is no less prevalent today than it was yesterday. Let us not confuse metamorphosis with de-sacralization.

Birth, life, and death are still crucial. We still cross that lonesome valley by ourselves. The sovereign, shaman, priest, and warrior are all with us—in different guises, with different names.

Some call today's hierophony "magico-religious paraphernalia" and brand-new rituals "sheer travesty" of the sacred. Yet many who practice such rituals still believe life has a sacred origin and eternal meaning. There is still a reality that transcends but that is manifested in this world. Men still stay close to their gods—even if some are not willing to recognize, let alone baptize, them. Look around you. *Homo religiosus* has not disappeared in our de-sacralized world: he is alive and well in his new electronic environment.

We have met him before, in a different context, as Traditional Man. We pointed out that he was radically related to a pre-scientific reality, that he depended on lore rather than academic learning, that he drew substance from nature, not media, and that he put his hopes in people, not machines.

Centuries later, in the football stadium, he understands well what he sees. The beast (football) is loose, and someone must capture it. Muscles, determination, and will power make all the difference. The struggle is primordial.[3]

He may even see a little blood—not makeup, as in the movies or on television. Real blood. Real pain.

That is why, as Super Bowls come and go, preparing for the game itself becomes more and more important. Starting in 1976, we have had a hallowed evening (Hallowe'en?) celebration on Saturday night . . . what the networks call "Supernight before Super Bowl." Well-known hosts (shamen?) are in charge, exhorting famous groups of comedians, singers, vestal virgins. Through the magic of film, we drift back to earlier Super Bowls

—"celebrity watching in cameo appearances." Former gridiron greats sing popular songs (like "Bad, Bad Leroy Brown") badly. No one wants to hear from, or listen to, the unbelievers, like Dave Meggysey, the St. Louis Cardinal linebacker who quit the game with these sour words:

> Football is an attempt to sell a blown-out, smacked-out people the notion that the system is still viable. Pro football keeps telling them they can't be second rate, they must win. No matter who you victimize or sacrifice, it's all worth it to be Number One.

For several years straight, the Pittsburgh Steelers were Number One, running their dynastic hold up to four in 1980. Over 100,000 people (superfans) packed the Pasadena Stadium, paying as much as $400 a ticket. Television commercials sold for $468,000 per minute, which works out to about $2,000 for every syllable. Had the United States been invaded during game time, as one commentator pointed out, millions of Americans would have been too preoccupied to notice. Players on both sides were given large cash bonuses; the victorious Steelers were given memorial rings—made not of steel, you may be sure, but of solid gold. The sacred ring—another ancient tie with religious ritual.

America seems to need football. When a hundred million people watch the Super Bowl on television, you *know* people need something to identify with.

You also know that someone will be around to turn a fast buck. (Jesus ran into the problem—the money changers whom he drove out of the Temple.) Before the 1981 contest between Oakland and Philadelphia, a nationwide black market in Super Bowl tickets surfaced. Millions of dollars were involved, along with players, coaches, team officials, and scalpers. Single tickets with a face value of forty dollars were selling for $500 or more. "This," one player was honest enough to admit, "is where we make the big score."

An investigation by the *Los Angeles Times* uncovered a vast labyrinth of buyers, runners, and sellers. Ticket scalpers and travel agents had organized ticket captains throughout the league's twenty-eight teams. Runners were recruited to fly from team to team, carrying large amounts of cash to bargain for whatever tickets were available. "Cash for tickets—no questions asked," was the runner's slogan. And lo, the cash did flow.

These tickets then started up the ladder, from scalper to broker to buyer. Sometimes they made possible Super Bowl tours underwritten by corporate giants. The business of America, Calvin Coolidge once remarked, is business. In a sports culture, whatever the state of the economy, it is business as usual.

Sometimes matters get out of hand. One veteran of Super Scalp 1980 recalled: "I walked to the gate to find 3,000 angry people on the curb—down from Pittsburgh with no tickets. There was a lot of rioting. Hotels on the beach got torn up. Blood flowed." What's a good ritual without a little blood?

Over the years, the magic: Super Sunday dawns. Ten thousand times ten thousand, a mighty army, go to the Bowl itself. Millions more witness the event on television screens, "against the beautiful skyline of _____." The destiny-laden pregame coin flip (the coin, incidentally, is worth $4,000) sets the scene. Players come onto the field, amid acclamations louder than any heard outside ancient Jerusalem's walls. They run, collide, bruise, bash. Now for the halftime festivities. Lines of young people march forth, precise as pistons in a well-tuned engine . . . females in yellow or orange, males in blue, teeth shining as they sing, "It's a Good Time to Know Your Neighbor." They form magic patterns, so they can better venerate the earth goddess America.

Then the superdrum, complete with cabalistic sign (NFL). Four priest warriors dance on the drumhead/godhead. The 100,000 worshippers are on their feet, tears in their eyes, singing:

> America, America,
> God shed his grace on thee. . . .

Amen.

NOTES

1. Michael Real, "The Super Bowl: Mythic Spectacle," in *Mass-Mediated Culture* (New York: Prentice-Hall, 1977), p. 76.

2. Clues to this search can be found in James Michener's *Sports in America* (New York: Scribners', 1978), and in such magazines as *Sports Illustrated*.

3. That games are a basic element to all cultures, no one doubts; but few of the games in modern popular culture have been carefully studied in a large context. The problem is explored in *The Study of Games* by E. M. Avedon and B. Sutton-Smith (New York: E. P. Dutton, 1970).

FURTHER READING

Avedon, E. M., and Sutton-Smith, B. *The Study of Games* (New York: E. P. Dutton, 1971).

Coffin, Tristram P. *The Old Ball Game: Baseball in Folklore and Fiction* (New York: Simon & Shuster, 1971).

Guttman, Allen. *From Ritual to Record: The Nature of Modern Sports* (New York: Columbia University Press, 1977).

Lipsyte, Robert. *Sports World: An American Dreamland* (New York: Quadrangle, 1975).

Manchester, Herbert. *Four Centuries of Sport in America* (New York: Hill and Wang, 1931).

14
COUNTER CULTURE

A cap of good acid costs five dollars. For
that you can hear the Universal Symphony, with
God singing solo and the Holy Ghost on drums.

Hunter Thompson

"In a democracy," Alexis de Tocqueville wrote in the 1830s,
"the majority has the chain in its hand." Eventually, many
American youths wanted to be unchained. They were fed up
with parents following the panicky ways of prestige, enslaved
to credit cards, cars, and canned culture. "Hell, no, we won't
go!"

The time of the Great Against. Not only against the Establish-
ment, the Man, racism, Vietnam, poverty, parents, but also

against God, grandmothers, mass media, virginity, and apple pie. (Two favorite buttons of the 1960s read: "Stamp Out Virginity" and "Apple Pie Makes You Sterile.") The time of Great Expectations.

Revolts against the Man (or king, state, party) go far back in history. Christianity was such a revolt; to better-class Romans, the catacomb crews must have looked like hippies. The free-swinging troubadors offended many a medieval household. The romantic "wanderers" of nineteenth-century Europe—especially in Germany—got wide notoriety and attention. But in the America of J. Edgar Hoover and *Readers' Digest*?

One key to the 1950s was conformity. In the Age of Eisenhower, historians said that most of our past conflicts were actually hyperbolic ritual warfare associated with politics. In due time, sensible moderate solutions by the Jeffersons, Lincolns, and Roosevelts always prevailed. The ship of state was moving steadfastly forward. Once insignificant English colonies became the leader of the Free World. The man who led the crusade to free Europe was in the White House (or on the golf course).

Meanwhile, back in the rec room, we had Elvis Presley, Pat Boone, and Johnny Mathis. Vladimir Nabokov's girlchild-heroine Lolita liked "sweet hot jazz . . . gooey fudge sundaes . . . movie magazines, and juke boxes with records made by people with names like Sammy and Jop and Eddy and Tony and Peggy and Guy and Patty and Rex."

As the silent 1950s became the swinging 1960s, the youth-quake flourished. By 1963, 6 million young people had bought guitars, and 11 million more regularly watched *Hootenanny*.

Youth hailed the election of President John F. Kennedy. His assassination shook the culture. This was followed by a whole series of killings and disasters. America was *not* "one nation, indivisible." It was at war with the world, even itself. All this—but most of all Vietnam—split the nation in two.

It was the first pop culture war, the first wired for instant sight and sound. The crucial fact was not so much the movement of troops as the placement of cameras. The day's war came with our dinner dessert. Allowing for a few days missed and Sundays off for the evening newscasters, Vietnam came into our house on over 3,000 evenings—around-the-calendar bombardment. Jerzy Kosinski summed it up in *Being There:*

"Have you served in the army?"
"No, I have seen the army on TV."

After World War I, *Farewell to Arms;* after Vietnam, farewell to innocence. Living in America wasn't fun any more. The "for fun" youth culture faded into the "for real" counter culture. Instead of high school proms and pig roasts, we had hard-core porn and "roast the pigs."

A full-scale *Credo* came when Students for a Democratic Society met in Port Huron, Michigan, in 1962. Widely applauded and quoted, it might have been labeled *Rousseau Revisited.* Power rooted in possession and privilege would be replaced by "power and uniqueness rooted in love, reason, and creativity." The most revealing passage of the manifesto was *On Man:*

We regard man as infinitely precious and possessed of unfulfilled capacities for reason, freedom, and love. In affirming these principles we are aware of countering the dominant conceptions of man in the twentieth century: that he is a thing to be manipulated, and that he is inherently incapable of directing his own affairs.

Grand talk: there were seamier sides to the revolution. Edward Lee Russell, a district health officer, complained that "the trend away from good personal hygiene" was having startling effects. Tests in three Anaheim, California, public schools turned up head lice in 1,500 students.

Youth produced a savior in Ken Kesey, and disciples in his Merry Pranksters. Kesey invited comparison to Christ, Allah, and Superman. He dressed Western, in a buckskin shirt with an open neck, copper-colored corduroy pants, red Mexican boots and a lambskin jacket. Wherever Kesey and the Pranksters were, there was a riot of flag costumes and dayglo—designs that looked like they came out of a comic book tradition rather than the temple at Karnak. There was a great electronic turbulence: of rock and roll, tapes, videotapes, amplifiers, theater horns, motion pictures, the wonderworld of modern recording and broadcasting.

In such an electronic spectacle, sounds, smells, sights innundate—squawks and squeaks like the short-wave radio from Vladivostok in a storm. Bang bang, big beat, hailstones falling, and bodies starting to grind. Herky-jerky motion: early silent films wired up to blastoff. Echoing electronic chambers, raw melodies riding computers bareback.

The spectacle is protean, readily assuming new shapes and roles. De Tocqueville's "motley multitude" has gone mad.

Spectacles are more aural and visual than verbal—sights and sounds penetrate more quickly than words. The mind isn't so much a debating society as a picture gallery. Icons are no longer at the altar but on the tube: behold the NBC peacock and CBS's Big Eye. Look at America as free action, pure game, dreams or architecture of dreams . . . the universe becoming *spectacle*, man becoming at once both spectacle and spectator.

The climax came in 1968 when over 400,000 of the liberated headed for Max Yasgur's 600-acre farm near Woodstock, New York. What happened at Woodstock? Aquarians grooved on acid-rock songs of innocence—so surpassingly strong that no one minded the torrential rains. A participant reported: "Everyone swam nude in the lake. Balling was easier than getting breakfast. Wow." Abbie Hoffman quickly wrote a best-seller called *Woodstock Nation.*

Weeds grow now where late the hard rocks sang. In its 1976 bicentennial issue, *Life* chose Woodstock as one of "The 100 Events that Shaped Ameirca." A "nation" of young found solace and inspiration in each other, a hypnotic sense of peace and elation. Was it a religious pilgrimage—a children's crusade? Perhaps. Tens of thousands still carry the Woodstock memory as a talisman in the years since they tramped back to a changing world . . . never to return.

Woodstock represented the skyrocket approach to dissent; much more enduring were a series of movements in which individuals studied, campaigned, and met for months or years to further some cause whose time had come. They were not so newsworthy or photogenic as the mass rallies and orgies, but they changed the culture in deeper and more lasting ways.

In the mid-1960s, feminists undertook a full-scale investigation of the status, role, and treatment of women, past and present. Within a few years, women's studies programs were under way in scores of universities and research centers. There had been important isolated studies earlier, such as Mary Beard's *Woman as a Force in History* (1946) and Viola Klein's *The Feminine Character: History of an Ideology* (1946). Repositories of women's materials and manuscripts were even older, such as the Sophia Smith Collection at Smith College and the Women's Archives at Radcliffe College. But a women's *movement*, affecting everyday economics, politics, and life-style, began only in the 1960s. Communication networks, lobbies, consciousness-raising groups, resource centers, and feminist presses came into being. A multivolume *Female Studies* was launched. Traditional sources were reexamined, and fresh sources were utilized. A decade later, the "movement" was a reality, a force to reckon with, on various levels, in contemporary America.

As always, that reality opened the door to fantasy. Alongside Superman, Wonder Woman became a cult-figure in the 1960s—the ultimate defender of women's rights. This comic book Amazon had been trained to believe that men are inherently evil. Charles M. Marston, the psychologist who invented Wonder Woman in 1942, wanted her to be an inspiring heroine for girls; a generation later, she became a psychic spokeswoman not only for girls but also for the women of America.

Some "movements" have wide impact so that historians can set specific dates as to beginning, flowering, decline. The black movement in America bears the opening date of 1954 because of the historic Supreme Court desegregation decision. Full of conflict and argument, the "movement" involved demonstrations, riots, confrontations, and the assassination of the chief black leader, Martin Luther King, Jr. Since then, progress has been less visual and vocal. The acceptance of its basic major premises had by 1980 become "mainstream" in American thinking and reacting.

Brought to the New World in bondage, blacks were first

assumed and then forced to be inferior. Afro-Americans were turned into stereotypes and shufflin' fools. A Cincinnati white man, Thomas Rice, blackened his face in 1839, donned a porter's costume, and mimicked black action and speech. Thus was born the Jim Crow stereotype, which lasted for generations. "People tend to treat Negroes like objects," pop singer Bob Dylan commented in 1969. Six years earlier, black writer LeRoi Jones noted that his ancestors were brought to a culture that was "the complete antithesis of one's own version of man's life on earth." The resulting cultural problems were enormous.[2]

The black contribution—especially in the area of popular culture—was also enormous. Work songs, spirituals, jazz, the blues are only the most obvious examples. The heritage and genius of black Americans reach back beyond 1619, when the first slaves were brought here. History was still blind when Africans forged powerful traditions, rhythms, and ceremonies —popular art in the fullest sense. Much of it was primitive in the sense of being primary—not of being crude or naive. Some of the most powerful rhythms of the twentieth century can be traced back to Africa.

My generation of art students was reared on Oliver W. Larkin's Pulitzer prize-winning text, *Art and Life in America*. Looking at it, I note that the word "black" does not appear in Larkin's detailed index except as part of three picture titles.[3] There are four brief references to "Negro craftsman" but none for "Negro artists," "Negro art," or "Negro influence."

It is difficult to produce a portrait of a collective identity. Art and life are not separated by any innate quality of value, only by particular standards we impose. Art can never be encompassed by canons of personal taste, but only as products of man the maker.[4] As toolmaker, homemaker, imagemaker, mythmaker, and citymaker, man uses his hands, head, heart to bring meaning out of chaos. This is the central truth on which culture is based.

Where does *American* black common culture begin? At the place and time when black men began to live, breathe, and create on American soil. Much of it was neither preservable nor preserved—mainly oral, not written; casual, not formal;

clandestine, not overt. What amazes us is how much was passed down.

In the second half of the twentieth century, circumstances improved. Integration and equality became the law of the land. Black scholar Saunders Redding advocated multiracial coopera- tion inside the framework of traditional scholarly disciplines. Others (like LeRoi Jones, who changed his name to Imamu Amiri Baraka) adopted a black nationalist philosophy. Seeing the United States as the world center of capitalism and racism, Baraka preached "self determination for the Afro-American nation in the black belt South." Where the "movement" would go in the years ahead, no one could be sure.[5]

Nor could one measure the impact of the counter culture on the popular arts—especially theater, music, and painting. With the 1967 production of *Hair* by Joseph Pass, a new kind of entertainment surfaced: a do-it-yourself earth ritual, complete with altar, sacred fire, and self-adjusting litany. No set lines— the script is a framework. *Do your thing.* Not only six troupes in the United States, but performances in fourteen countries. *Hair* is a way of life. Galt MacDermot's music with lyrics by Gerome Ragni and James Rado. Their rock-style lingo translates into any language. The Japanese, busted for possessing marijuana, dis- played poetic emotions. Another memorable event occurred in Toronto when a white girl with silky blonde tresses knelt humbly to shine the shoes of a black girl with her hair.

The psychedelic and drug phase of the youth explosion began in 1960, when Timothy Leary "turned on" Allen Ginsberg, a former student-turned-poet. Leary related how the two planned to sell the new psychedelic revolution; Leary, with his impres- sive academic credentials, would line up influential prospects so that on weekends they could spread the Good News: drugs, not prayers, were the road to salvation.

A "theology of counter culture" emerged. Intelligent and articulate people conceived and spread it. The spectacle of drug addicts and casualties should not obscure the magic of those heady days.

In Leary's view, the human mind is like a telephone switchboard: organized, programmed to make specific connections. A certain signal comes in, and the mind plugs in to a predictable reaction. It is usually boring because most people's minds have been programmed in a routine way. Society has programmed them. Their families have programmed them with routine responses, conventional reactions, which they got from *their* families. The school system hooks in a few more predictable circuits. Churches, governments, institutions, organizations hook in some more, routine and mass produced. The mass media keep the whole boring piece of circuitry in good, tight, clean, rustproof, standardized shape. Anyone who puts a penny in the fuse box goes off to the funny farm. All men end up with the same braincircuit, the same conventional pattern. It is but one of millions of ways in which the brain leaving home fleeced them on the West Coast. Merchants discovered that by attaching "psychedelic" or "acid" to any merchandise allowed instant markups. They changed the words (but kept the markups) for every protesting ethnic group, political crusader, and feminist. It was the old story: gullible sheep being led to the slaughter.

Magazines and books reflect the mood and the shallowness of the time. *Evergreen* and *Ramparts* developed their own visual clichés, such as the eagle killing the dove ("military-industrial complex") and the pig carrying a rifle ("police state"). Not the Communists but the CIA became the ultimate villain. For a group of young writers, that villain was the school system. Their efforts got wide attention—books like Paul Goodman's *Growing Up Absurd* (1960), John Holt's *Compulsary Mis-education* (1964), Jonathan Kozol's *Death at an Early Age* (1967), and Jerry Farber's *The Student as Nigger* (1969).

But it is wrong to pick out a few books as "trendy," "flaky," or "dated," without pointing out that thousands of people, in all walks of life, capitalized consciously or unconsciously on the mood of those turbulent days. I can remember watching on my television screen big-city stores being looted—no one dared to stop them. I can also remember attending national meetings of the Popular Culture Association and seeing the dissidents stream in, replete with hound dogs, guitars, and groupies, ready and willing to "do their thing." The Great Youth Hustle! Half the population was under twenty-five; those over thirty were admonished to keep quiet. Youth had become a nation set apart . . . a rallying sign . . . a secret signal . . . a billion-dollar market for clothes, records, jewelry, trinkets, posters, trendy magazines, porn, whole lines of psychedelic goods and gifts. Anyone interested could move about America and document it.

One of the best summaries is William L. O'Neill's *Coming Apart: An Informal History of America in the 1960's* (1972). "Standards decayed," he writes. "A nation caught up in a manic-depressive cycle was trying at both extremes. Yet this was not a people to write off too soon. Life was in them yet, and with it, hope."[6] "Apocalypse was in the air in the late 1960's," Robert Sobel added in *The Manipulators* (1976). "The temptation to use media pulpits to preach and exhort was greater than any other time."

Then, suddenly, it was all over. Whatever happened to the 1960s? Historians may ask the question for decades to come and never find the anwer. As for popular culture studies: less hair and blare; more talk of theory and methodology. Perhaps this is as it must be. The world is still Darwinian, only the species that adapt to new circumstances survive.

Since World War II, raw-boned survival has been cloaked by a peculiarly American phenomenon: abundance. One could say of our whole society what Shakespeare had a shrewd observer say of Caesar:

> Upon what meat doth this our Caesar eat
> That he hath grown so fat?

A country wracked in the post-Nixon years with inflation, unemployment, and natural calamities found out that the cornucopia does not pour out goodies forever. The three religions that have most shaped modern civilization (Christianity, Judaism, and Islam) came out of the desert—out of fasting, famine, and poverty. Holy men in all ages scorn earthly excesses, mortify their bodies, denounce opulent neighbors. John the Baptist's wardrobe consisted largely of animal skins, his diet of grasshoppers. Jesus said that the poor are always with us and went to the desert to fast and pray. Self-denial remains the most impressive gesture a leader can make. India's independence came when Mahatma Gandhi refused to eat. A generation later, the hunger strikes and deaths in Northern Ireland had enormous impact around the world.

Over the centuries, the idea that wickedness is the handmaiden of abundance has been widely accepted. Since there never has been enough to go around, anyone with extra portions must have either inherited it (he is undeserving) or appropriated it (he is unloving). History records the unending struggle to overthrow kings, robber barons, and tyrants—to see that government is run for the many, not the few. But what happens when (to quote Emerson), "Things are in the saddle/And ride mankind?" What happens when abundance becomes a mindset —a national consciousness, bolstered by government, business, education, and mythology?

Charles Reich attempts to answer in *The Greening of America*, one of the spring blooms in 1971. "We may be in the grip not of capitalist exploiters," he writes, "but of mindless, impersonal forces that pursue their own, non-human logic." Never mind, Reich counsels, the machine will self-destruct. The chromobile, fabulously expensive and instantly obsolete, will not prevail.

Reich is wrong. The revolution is more basic than the one he posits. Consciousness I and II may well give way to III, and then IV—but the wheels will not stop rolling. People will *drive* to Woodstock. Many other "revolutions" of our times—happenings and minimal art, black or red liberation, America and counter culture may or may not outlast their highly vocal founders. But these wheels. . . .

What the mounting energy crises of the 1970s indicated was that fads come and go, but myths die hard. Automobiles have become a deep-seated part of our mythology. In them, we perform the rites of passage: separation, initiation, return. The car has refashioned all the spaces that unite and separate our people. We cannot, we will not, concede those spaces.

Nor can anyone deny the creative vigor and verve of those counter-culture years. Think of music, film, journalism, ritual— youth around the world responded to America's beat and has been doing so ever since. Large groups of people, including millions of females, sought and achieved new levels of freedom and involvement. Few decades in American life have left so large a legacy.

And few have seen so much trauma for so many so quickly. A rock group called the Moody Blues serves as a metaphor. In 1969, these five young musicians earned over $20 million. They were the first rock group invited to perform in Red China. They announced that they were building a $1.5 million recording studio near London—the most advanced and sophisticated in the world.

Five years later, they were bankrupt. Frantic efforts to make another hit album failed. "It wasn't working," their spokesman John Edge said. "We were hoping we could make it through. All the pressures finally got to us." The *New York Times* carried this headline: A Requiem for the Moody Blues.

Judgments on the counter culture and its derring-do have been mainly negative.[7] Many thought it one of the sloppier public myths of the American middle class. Studies showed how shallow the causes had been, how theatrical the threats, how commercial the orientation. Madison Avenue turned out to be the big winner. It adopted the unbeatable strategy: if you can't lick 'em, join 'em.

With the 1960s and 1970s behind us, Paul Dolan and Edward Quinn try to catch *The Sense of the 70's*:

> It was a time of retreat to a past that was safer, more secure. Nostalgia covered the land like a maternal blanket. It is as though we had become conscious of time and were engaged in some desperate effort to hold it back.[8]

But every once in a while, when you hear a wild shout in the night, and music from a guitar, and the lyrics of an early Bob Dylan tune. . . .

NOTES

1. See J. S. Zangrando, "Women's Studies in the United States: Approaching Reality." *American Studies International* (Winter 1971).

2. LeRoi Jones, *Blues People* (New York: William Morrow, 1963), p. 1. See also Douglas A. Hughes, *From a Black Perspective* (New York: Holt, Rinehart, and Winston, 1970).

3. Larkin's book was published in 1949 and reprinted in 1960. I am not implying that Larkin was a racist or a bigot: he reflected the time in which he lived and worked.

4. This point is developed in anthropological writings. See Melville Herskovits, *Man and His Works* (New York: Knopf, 1948).

5. See Jefferson B. Kellogg, "Redding and Baraka: Two Contrasting Views of Afro-American Studies," *American Studies International* 17, no. 4 (Summer 1979). This publication contains a long bibliography on "The Black Revolution."

6. William L. O'Neill. *Coming Apart: An Informal History of America in the 1960's* (Chicago: Quadrangle, 1971), p. 242.

7. Some of the old apologists hang on. See Theodore Roszak's *The Aquarian Frontier and the Evolution of Consciousness* (New York: Harper & Row, 1976) and Jim Hougan's *Radical Nostalgia, Narcissism, and Decline in the Seventies* (New York: William Morrow, 1976).

8. Paul Dolan and Edward Quinn, *The Sense of the Seventies* (New York: Oxford University Press, 1978), p. 13.

FURTHER READING

Dolan, Paul J., and Quinn, Edward. *The Sense of the Seventies* (New York: Oxford University Press, 1978).

Hayes, Harold, ed. *Smiling Through the Apocalypse: Esquire's History of the Sixties* (New York: McCall's, 1969).

London, Herbert I. *The Overheated Decade* (New York: New York University Press, 1976).

Reich, Charles. *The Greening of America* (New York: Random House, 1970).

Roszak, Theodore. *The Making of a Counter Culture* (New York: Doubleday, 1969).

Slater, Philip. *The Pursuit of Loneliness* (Boston: Beacon Press, 1970).

Wolfe, Tom. *The Kandy Kolored Tangerine Flake Streamline Baby* (New York: Simon and Schuster, 1965).

15
CONSENSUS CULTURE

We keep meeting each other, and we recognize
each other; we know we are the traveling
pioneers of the new age.

Jonas Mekas

Behold Rome—mighty and majestic, sacked and dying, parched
and polluted; the Eternal City and Eternal Asylum for anybody
from anywhere who is looking for the lost past.

Rome, the timeless refugee camp for pilgrims, saints, tourists,
scholars, filmmakers, hippies, hucksters. City of gloomy catacombs, crumbling walls, gushing fountains. Homemakers, girl-
makers, leg breakers: their paths converge here. A good place to
see what is left of the old common culture and what can be
salvaged for the new.

In any season, one sniffs the distant smell of death. When the flesh has rotted, white bones become building blocks of idolotry and mythology. Rome, once the hub of the greatest empire in history, is the boneyard of our common heritage.

Boneyard? Rome is bursting with creative energy and unrest. No designers surpass the Italians in clothes, shoes, automobiles, graphics. The cinema is superb. Every year, 2.5 million comic books pour from the press. Television, opera, and theater flourish. Italy is full of wonderful actors—but most are never on stage.

Layer on layer of history—all under a coat of brown dust. Old ladies wipe it off their faces as they push into markets . . . lean and alone, pushing to get their overripe peaches. The streets are full of men, machines, and motion. Their 1909 *Futurist Manifesto* was an early attempt to baptize popular culture; the roles of Gino Severini, Umberto Boccioni, Giorgio Morandi, and Alberto Savinio have been underestimated.[1] I will toast them, looking down on the Roman Forum, swarming with tired tourists and criminal cats. I will ask myself: What is there that makes this past such an unmistakable part of the twentieth century? How could the culture that defied Hannibal and the Golden Horde be won by Coca-Cola? Why are all these ruins wired for sound? Why do Italian babies fall asleep clutching plastic Mickey Mouses?

Italy: Haven for priests, plastics, popular culture. The Iron Curtain doesn't keep out sounds and images. The same beat London swings to is heard in Moscow and Budapest. And wait till you hear them sing country and western music in Tokyo!

This is not a naive statement about the Brotherhood of Man or the universality of Love-Ins. Old racial and ethnic struggles continue, aggravated by verbal and electronic overkill. Old-style hate-baiting politicians continue to divide us, but they will not prevail. Something's afoot in the universe. In the late twentieth century, an unprecedented merging and blending of sights, sounds, and meanings are taking place. Premodern elements (primitivism, superstitions, meditation, occultism) give the flavor of old "common culture." But time never runs backward, and the differences in the postmodern electronic era are so great that a new label is needed. Call it *consensus culture.*

Consensus (from Latin *consentire*, to feel together, to agree) implies a coming together of divergent data. In terms of space and time (two words now joined into the single concept of space-time), the convergence is unmistakable. We are adrift on Barbara Ward's "spaceship earth."

Other parts of the world—empires, ideologies, arts, populations, platitudes—are linking and regrouping in novel ways. Not only people but movements flash like meteors across well-monitored skies.

Can confusion give way to consensus?

An intriguing question, this. The idea of consensus and unity (in village, city, region, nation, world) is as old as humanity itself, affecting art, religion, and philosophy. People everywhere have prayed "that we may be all of one heart, and of one soul, with one mind and one mouth." In the 1970s, that dream centered around the global village.

History was unrecorded when multitudes dreamed and died for a unity they were not destined to achieve. Ancient warrior-conquerors have long receded into legend or limbo. The poet Shelley summed it up when he described "two vast and trunkless legs of stone" standing in the endless desert, with this inscription:

> My name is Ozymandias, king of kings;
> Look on my works, ye Mighty, and despair!

Some leaders and empires fared better. In the spring of 334 BC, Alexander the Great swept into Asia. In eleven years, he conquered the civilized world and established his empire. In those same years, a youth named Zeno grew up in Cypress, founded Stoicism, and taught that all men are common citizens of the same world-state. Thus, the concept of universal citizenship was well established centuries before the Christian epoch.

We shall not herald conquerors that swept over Asia, Africa, and Europe. Each was himself conquered; even the mighty Roman Empire, which gave the world a *pax Romana* and an internal unity surpassing any other in history, was pulled apart by dissenters within and invaders without. No military and political system has ever been able to eliminate all diversity and dissent.

No religion has ever converted men everywhere to its doctrines. "Let us sit on the ground," Shakespeare wrote, "and tell sad tales of the death of kings."

The universalism of the Roman world, rooted in Greek civilization but free of the exclusiveness of its state, prepared the West for universal Christianity, rooted in Judaism but free of the ethnic exclusiveness of Israel. Roman Christianity, proclaimed by Constantine in the fourth century AD and later formalized in the papacy, shaped "one world doctrine" that dominated Western civilization for centuries before the emergence of nationalism and the *Staatensystem*.

The Holy Roman Empire, a powerful and persuasive view of the global village as European Christians then understood it, lasted 1,000 years, finally falling to the French revolutionary armies of Napoleon in the early nineteenth century. A French empire then appeared, followed by an even more majestic British empire. ("The sun never sets on British soil.") The political and military might of European colonial powers quickly faded in the following century. During their zenith, a different kind of event—the Electronic Revolution—took place.

Arguments abound as to just when and where it began. Benjamin Franklin was performing his electrical experiments before our nation was born; major steps occurred in the eighteenth century. Yet the dramatic appearance of the Three T's (telegraph, telephone, typewriter) in the nineteenth century was the crucial breakthrough. The telegraph gave us a social nervous system, divorced from "muscle culture." For centuries, the only way to carry messages long distances was at the speed of a human or a horse. By making information available instantaneously, the telegraph ended the dependency of communication on physical transportation. It became the control model and paradigm for a new cosmology.

Messages were telegraphed around Europe in the 1850s and across the Atlantic in 1866. The telephone was conceived shortly thereafter, predicating the modern industrial word.

The coming of radio at the turn of the century made possible simultaneous communication between some central authority and any number of receivers. Broadcasting, supplementing an already widespread press, created mass communication. In one step, the speed at which messages could be sent was increased *some 10 million times*: in effect, there was NO time delay.

For sheer inventiveness, electronics has no equal in history. Consider this fact: a man could have lived from the advent of the telephone to the landing of a man on the moon. During that period, he would have seen the birth of atomic power, television, the space age.

For most of us, who neither dropped atomic bombs nor walked on the moon, the *real* breakthrough, day after day, is television. We have already noted, in chapter 5, the similarity between television and dreams, with their multiple fantasies. Crossing language, ethnic, age, sexual, and national boundaries effortlessly and simultaneously, television is far more than a dream machine. It is a giant industry, a continuous production belt—a "sausage machine" that must be fed day after day, so as to produce right things at right times on right channels. Television is by far the most popular art; a crucially important object of study, Horace Newcomb points out, "not only because it is a new form, a different medium, but because it brings its massive audience into a direct relationship with particular sets of values and attitudes";[2] *the* archetype of mass communication in the late twentieth century. To discuss television is to discuss the society that sponsors and creates it. If there is to be a genuine consensus, it will be viable and visible on television.

We have long known that people need rituals, myths, and totems to enjoy consensus and have assumed that, in our rational scientific blessedness, all these things have disappeared. We never yell for the bulls and bears (except on Monday night televised football) and do not worship golden calves (except on Wall Street). Have these earlier modes slipped into our life via television? Is not the nightly CBS news a form of community worship? Was not Walter Cronkite (whose retirement as anchorman for CBS was a national event) a true high priest, keeper of the public conscience? Was it not *his* agonizing judgment that Richard Nixon was guilty that played a role in the only presidential resignation in our history?

There surely *is* the possibility that another name for the

emerging global life-style is "videoculture." It has already produced the largest group of people bound together in a single communication net in history. No one can yet say how that might soon be both enlarged and deepened by satellite, cable, public television, and various forms of home gadgetry.[3]

We entered outer space full of inner confidence: by then we had our computers. Devised during World War II, the first successful model was built at the University of Pennsylvania in 1946. Weighing thirty tons with 18,000 tubes, it could do an incredible 5,000 additions per second. Twenty years later, that rate had increased one thousand fold. But so, in some areas, had the problems.

If information could be gathered so quickly on such a vast scale, who should have access to what? What were the proper limits of privacy? If machines could do the work of people, what work should people do?

Wasn't it wonderful to have so many automobiles—but where would we park them? Were cities for people or for parking? What about pollution? And workers who did not *want* to spend their lives on assembly lines? Was the love affair with mass production waning?

Things long taken for granted could not be assumed to be the basis for consensus. Progress and production were no longer assumed goods. Western leadership was not inevitable and media expansion not everywhere acceptable. Too much modernism too quickly could be disastrous. The agony of Iran, which disrupted much of the world during the hostage crisis, was a clear example of how *not* to get workable consensus.

Hints came from the drama in oil-rich Iran, where the American-backed shah rushed precipitously into modern times and technology. Led by a religious fundamentalist, Ayatollah Khomeini, traditional Iranians overthrew the shah, then seized the American embassy when the United States allowed the shah to enter the country for medical aid. This event, staged on November 4, 1979, set off the longest hostage crisis in the twentieth century (444 days), preoccupied the international community, and threatened world peace.

With all her wealth, influence, and power, the American giant was helpless when a group of religious zealots pointed their government in the direction of ninth-century Islam. Under the values of that time, Iran had enjoyed a common culture and had partaken of a great tradition. By reviving it, the nation had become a tiny David, able to stop the mighty Goliath.

Did the hostage crisis cost Jimmy Carter the presidency and bring a career soldier to the post of secretary of state? What role was played in the drama by the continuous media coverage (including the ritualistic reminder of the number of days in captivity at the end of nightly news programs)? Did the humiliation of America serve as a kind of mini-Pearl Harbor, bringing patriotism back and raising flags on their poles? What lesson would similarly traditional Third World cultures learn from Iran's exploit?

Earlier, an electronic superstar had appeared on the horizon: Marshall McLuhan. By the mid-1970s, most critics and communicators believed that, despite the slickeries, trickeries, and peppery puns, McLuhan had misread history and had misunderstood the medium where he seemed most brilliant: television. Most critics were convinced, before McLuhan's death in 1980, that the role of content to television was crucial, just as it has been with the printing press and every other great innovation. Much new data indicated that McLuhan's writing was based on personal speculation, not observation.

Nor did time validate McLuhan's predictions about the interlocked monolithic global village. Witnessing ever-rising localism, regionalism, and nationalism, some denounced the global village metaphor; we were seeing instead the balkanization of the world. In the April 1974 issue of *Mass Comm Review*, Everette E. Dennis published his "Post-Mortem on McLuhan:"

His books attract little comment in 1974. Not since 1970 has the *New York Times* had an article on him. He was an intellectual celebrity serving some social utility.

After McLuhan, a different kind of scholar-theorist came into prominence—social scientists who depended on thorough research, quantitative analysis, and numerical accuracy. The best were not afraid to theorize. A case in point is Jeremy Tunstall, whose book *The Media Are American* set forth the doctrine of media imperialism.

In most of McLuhan's global village, as Tunstall pointed out, the media are there only because of American enterprise. That includes not only the hardware but also the style and patterns that most countries have adopted and copied. "This influence," he writes, "includes the very definition of what a *newspaper, feature film*, or *television set* is." The high tide of American media lasted from 1943 to 1953:

> By 1953 the conquered nations were starting to go their own way again. Chronic shortages of media materials of all kinds were beginning to ease. 1953 marks a shift from direct to more indirect American media influence on the world.[4]

A whole library of materials and theories on the global village and spaceship earth was accumulating, much of it faddish and ephemeral. Martin E. Marty published "How to Tell a Fad from a Trend." No one ever thinks *he* is faddish; fads are other people's obsessions. "For one terrifying moment," Marty writes, "we thought theology was to be done over the telephone or television." Why not? Why are print-oriented people so "terrified" when other media appear? Why do critics like McLuhan enrage them? Perhaps that most unusual Roman Catholic theologian, Pierre Teilhard de Chardin, gave the best answer. With the acceleration of change, those who make scientific sense about the future are not the realists but the utopians.

In 1976, *Decline of the Global Village* appeared. Editor James Grunig said we have all experienced a taste of the global village and have come to realize that media do not heed national boundaries and restrictions. But what happens to the needs of primary groups, subgroups, and specific communities in the global village? McLuhan does not provide a satisfactory answer to that question. "He does not account for the communication vacuum induced by global interrelationships and a situation in which communication channels are monopolized by the few."[5]

Certainly people everywhere are being bombarded, caressed, fondled, swayed, narcotized, entertained, and taught by the mass media. The grand theories of McLuhan, Barbara Ward, Buckminster Fuller, William I. Thompson, and others provide only a partial explanation of media process and impact. They forget that monopoly of media and knowledge creates new media. Harold A. Innis suggests in *The Bias of Communication* that a stable society is dependent on an appreciation of a proper balance between the concepts of space and those of time. The key word is *balance*. Changes already under way in many spheres (politics, economics, scholarship, creative arts) indicate that the world balance will change drastically in the 1980s, and with it, the whole concept of cultural unity.

Our postindustrial society is characterized by service industries that are consumers of specialized media, directed to smaller, more homogeneous audiences. Technological growth and increased wealth (much of it outside the West) provide the means necessary for developing these specialized media. The trend is toward specialization in magazines, radio, and television. The mass media are actually shrinking in size relative to the total economy.[6]

This suggests that we must study not only the mass media but all media and communications systems. Some have been largely neglected, like the telephone and telegraph. New media, such as the office communications system, have been slighted. The impact of smaller systems on the big ones has not been taken into account.

The individual is not simply the target for standardized messages coming from the mass media. He is a communicator with access to a powerful set of media tools, receiving a wide range of messages directed to him by others. Rather than becoming ever more standardized and homogenized, world cultures are becoming ever more differentiated.[7] We are moving farther from the world George Orwell predicted in *1984*.

Earlier accounts of the global village were too simplistic and superficial. They underestimated the power of tradition, separation, and autonomy. Most people are still living as did generations of their ancestors: in tribal, local, or national patterns.

These tight communities, despite media intrusions, cling to limited horizons and emotions. In all times and places, a handful have thought boldly and traveled widely. Most have known only a few people and have been buried close to the spot where they were born. The media revolution and analysis of the world is beyond their ken.

This is not to deny that millions have been bombarded by sights and sounds from faraway places, often in a foreign tongue. Facts that only a few years ago would have ben unavailable surround and envelop them. But as Colin Cherry points out from his vantage point as professor of telecommunication at the University of London, this may not be uniting people:

> The spread of world news may do as much to keep people apart, in their emotions and attitudes, as it does to keep them informed about facts. Our whole communication network may drive us apart emotionally just as it draws us together institutionally. It is grossly naive to assume that expanding world communication necessarily leads to peace and understanding.[8]

It can succeed only when it meets existing needs, strategies, and conditions. If and as it violates our sense of time and place— or our self-interest—the global village will fail. No nation or consortium of nations can hope to dominate the global village, where the emphasis will change from penetration to partnership.

Some long-term challenges are suggested by Michael Real in *Mass-Mediated Culture*. Our global village soon will have its own electronic global library—who will be allowed to check out what? Telesensory devices seem close at hand, as do logical languages and robots. Memory playback is a definite possibility and regular contact with extraterrestrials a haunting one. Do we dare predict when there will be a world brain?[9]

As new media (as well as models and improvements of the old) appear with stunning swiftness, nothing seems too far-fetched. The legal process cannot keep pace. Who can copy what, and when, on the new video recorders? What regulations apply to cable television and computer connections? Who should and can control supersonic travel? And all the objects orbiting the earth and cluttering up the heavens?

As always, it is more difficult to cope with human beings than with their artifacts. True, the world is wired for sound—but how does that sound to the people who are wired? Can and should we *force* people into the global village? Who should issue the passports?

These and many other vexing questions demand all the skill, knowledge, patience, and vision we can muster. Many will not be answered in this decade or century. As we move forward, we can record not only problems but also prospects. This has been a great century for Homo Sapiens—but a better one may be coming. Without referring to psychic and spiritual changes, we can see how many have come in the physical realm. In two decades, life expectancy in the developing world has jumped from forty-two to fifty years. The literacy rate has climbed from a third to a half and continues to soar. The "green revolution" has worked in many countries and will be tried in others. Tourism is expanding, and no one can yet measure or imagine its results.

Never has life on this planet been in such flux for so many. The dangers are great, but so are the opportunities. In some form or other, the global village may not be merely a concept but a possibility.

More and more writers and thinkers believe this. Geoffrey Barraclough concludes in his *Introduction to Contemporary History*:

> The European age is over, and with it the predominance of the old European values. The civilization of the future is taking shape as a world civilization.[10]

In that world civilization new attention is being paid to memory, learning, brain research, humanistic medicine, biofeedback, and creativity. Not only scholars but popularizers sense this. New Journalist Marilyn Ferguson produced a newsletter called *Brain/Mind Bulletin,* then a 1973 best seller on *The Brain Revolution.* This paved the way for a 1980 book which seems cultic for the 1980s as Reich's *The Greening of America* had been for the 70s. Ferguson's *The Aquarian Conspiracy: Personal and Social Transformation in the 1980s*, heralded a new mind—"a turnabout in consciousness in a critical number of individuals, a network powerful enough to bring about radical change to our culture."

Conspire, in its literal sense, means "to breathe together." Why an *Aquarian* conspiracy? In Marilyn Ferguson's words:

> Although I am unacquainted with astrological lore, I was drawn to the symbolic power of the pervasive dream of our popular culture: that after a dark, violent age, the Piscean, we are entering a millennium of love and light—in the words of the popular song, "The Age of Aquarius," the time of "the mind's true liberation."[11]

That our society must be remade, not just mended, is "a concept which has come into common usage." Common usage? Consensus culture? Common culture? Let the musing and the merging continue.

NOTES

1. See Giuseppi Marchiori, *Arte e artisti d'Avanguardia in Italia, 1910-1950* (Milano: Rizzardi, 1960), and John Canaday, *What Is Art?* (New York: Knopf, 1980), pp. 41 f.

2. Horace Newcomb, *TV: The Most Popular Art* (New York: Avon, 1975), p. 156, and *Television: The Critical View* (New York: Oxford, 1976). For television as an archetype, see Richard Hoggart, *Speaking to Each Other* (London: Chatto and Windus, 1970). The "inner workings" of network television are discussed in Robert Metz's *CBS: Reflections in a Bloodshot Eye* (Chicago: Playboy Press, 1975).

3. For details, see Colin Cherry, *World Communication: Threat or Promise?* (New York: John Wiley, 1978). See also N. D. Psurtsev, ed., *Development of Communication in the U.S.S.R.* (in Russian) (Moscow, 1967). This is a survey of fifty years, 1917-67.

4. Jeremy Tunstall, *The Media Are American* (New York: Columbia University Press, 1977), p. 136.

5. Gary Gumpert, "The Rise of Mini-Comm," in James Grunig, ed., *Decline of the Global Village* (Bayside, N.Y.: General Hall, 1976), p. 67.

6. This conclusion is documented by Richard Maisel, "The Decline of Mass Media," in Grunig, *Decline of the Global Village*, chapter 6.

7. To put it differently, we may need a three-stage rather than a two-stage theory to explain events in the global village. The idea is discussed in John Merril and Ralph Lowenstein, *Media, Message and Man* (New York: Hayden, 1971).

8. Cherry, *World Communication*, p. 175.

9. Michael R. Real, *Mass-Mediated Culture* (New York: 1977), chapter 1.

10. Geoffrey Barraclough, *Introduction to Contemporary History* (London: Penguin, 1976), p. 231.

11. Marilyn Ferguson, *The Aquarian Conspiracy: Personal and Social Transformation in the 1980s* (Los Angeles: J. P. Tarcher, 1980).

FURTHER READING

Grunig, James. *Decline of the Global Village* (Bayside, N.Y.: General Hall, 1976).

McLuhan, Marshall, with Quentin Fiore. *War and Peace in the Global Village* (New York: Bantam, 1968).

Newcomb, Horace. *TV: The Most Popular Art* (Garden City, N.Y.: Anchor Books, 1974).

Reichardt, Jasia. *Robots: Fact, Fiction, and Prediction* (New York: Penguin, 1978).

Servan-Schreiber, J. J. *The American Challenge* (New York: Avon, 1969).

Wells, H. G. *The Time Machine and The War of the Worlds* (New York: Oxford, 1977).

16
CLONING CLOWNS

God may or may not be dead, but Ronald
McDonald is immortal.

Jon Carroll

McDonald's is a microcosm of America—and of the emerging
consensus culture. We have seen the future, and it is dressed
like a clown.

His name, everyone knows, is Ronald McDonald. He has the
clownish traits: humor, honor, humility. He dances, prances,
and becomes one with little children. He loves hamburgers,
works magic, and defies gravity. Ronald is fast becoming iconic
as his image calls forth an army of ideas.

Clowns are older than recorded history; their origin is shrouded in mystery. Ritual clowning stretches back into primitive societies—perhaps into the caves. Wall paintings in tombs at Beni Hasan in the Nile Valley show that clowns, acrobats, and magicians were popular thousands of years before Christ. For centuries, itinerant clowns roamed and rollicked, evolving eventually into mountebanks, jesters, medicine show men, and nightclub comics. There were jugglers in Xanadu, acrobats in Crete, grotesques in Greece. Slapstick and buffoonery reigned in the Roman *fabulae togatea* and help ABC get top ratings in network struggles.[1]

Artists, historians, and theologians have rediscovered the clown in the atomic age. One leading theologian, Henri Nouwen, in *Clowning in Rome* (1979), helped to clarify their immortality. "They appear between the great acts," he writes, "fumble and fall, and make us smile again after the tensions created by the heroes we came to admire." The very fact that they do not have it together, but are awkward and out of balance, appeals to people for whom balance and grace are seldom seen. They draw from us not admiration but sympathy, not amazement but understanding. To *understand* the clown is a giant step toward *understanding* popular culture.

Clowns remind us that we share the same common culture and meet the same common terrors. "The longer I was in Rome," Nouwen continues, "the more I enjoyed the clowns, who by their humble lives evoke a smile and awaken hope."

What is a fair without a clown? Derived from the Latin *feria* (festival), the first fairs brought worshipers and pilgrims to sacred places, such as St. Bartholomew's in England. Clowns fill crucial roles in Shakespeare's plays and gained color and prominence in the Italian *commedia dell'arte*, an improvised art form. Ronald is a descendant of the *zanni*, or comic servants of the commedia, such as the sly and witty Harlequin and the awkward Pedrolino, whose costume of baggy trousers, loose fitting blouse, and wide brimmed or peaked hat is still won by most clowns.

The English pantomime theater, prominent in the eighteenth century, used these and other commedia characters. Gradually, the "clown" emerged, first as a stock supporting figure and later as a leading character with words and music. English actor Joseph Grimaldi (1778-1837) gave the clown a central importance and devised special white-faced makeup, accented with red paint. Both the role of "clown" or "joey" and the makeup Grimaldi developed were copied and introduced into the circus. They are with us still, on stage, screen, and television. Ronald has a goodly heritage.[2]

Not Ronald, but *Ronalds*—for McDonald's employs over a hundred now, even maintaining a school for them. Historical data self-destruct in our electronic age; we may not ever know just who conceived of Ronald. Groupthink came into play; Cooper and Golin, a major Chicago public relations firm, took over.

There is a prepackaged *Ronald McDonald Biography*, which corporate public affairs personnel mail upon request from McDonald's Plaza, Oak Brook, Illinois. The first Ronald (name unspecified) made his local debut in Washington, D.C., and his national debut a few months later—Macy's annual Thanksgiving Day Parade—New York City, November 28, 1963. His prop on that occasion was the world's largest drum. Who could have foreseen that within a decade Ronald would himself (or themselves) be the world's best publicized clown?

Ronald first appeared on network television in 1966, and other fantasy-characters were gradually added over the years. Most of them have been "toned down" since their original appearance. "Evil Grimace," for example, has become simply "Grimace," a lovable purple blob. The Hamburglar started as a frightening and mischievous fellow but has become a mere bungler. All this from the first scripts written by Needham, Harper, and Steers, McDonald's national advertising agency. Storylines are based on products and vary according to advertisement policy and need. Ronald has been dubbed "official spokesman" since 1967 and has filled that role admirably. More important, he has become a *living entity*, a *ding an sich*, for millions of people . . . a perpetual and immortal clown. His creators have proclaimed him "more famous than Lassie or the Easter Bunny." One may argue this, without denying that he is part of our media landscape; the genial host of McDonaldland, with all that implies.

What do his creators think about Ronald's prospects? "He has a very bright future with the McDonald's Corporation."[3]

Is McDonaldland modeled (consciously or unconsciously) on Disneyland? Is Ronald a Sorcerer's Apprentice who can turn the flow of hamburgers on but who cannot stop it? Does he even *want* to stop it? Or will he drive all other competitors, all other foods, out of the land? That is the Orwellian question.

Meanwhile, Ronald is intelligent and sensitive, but always clownlike. King Moody has been the television commercial "Ronald" since 1970. It is his face that most of us know and identify with the name; now he trains other Ronalds.[4] The other fantasy characters who surround him look up to and respect him; they complement, never upstage, Ronald Superstar.

What exactly does Ronald do? In the words of the "official biography":

> Ronald does everything kids would like to do—skating, boating, flying around in the air, magic, riding on camels and best of all, going to McDonald's to eat hamburgers, his favorite food. Ronald spends all his time going from one McDonald's restaurant to another to see his friends, the children. If his friends are sick he visits them at the hospital. Ronald's favorite thing to do is to make children happy, to make everyone laugh.

Ronald has delighted not only children but also adults who own McDonald's stock or work under the Golden Arches. Ronald chronicles "a modern commercial miracle," powered by a mighty munching army consuming billions of hamburgers around the world. Ronald symbolizes the world's most ubiquitous fast-food chain. But there is more to it than that, says Conrad Phillip Kottak, an anthropologist at the University of Michigan, in the January 1978 issue of *Natural History*:

> McDonald's has become nothing short of a secular religion, the shelter below the Golden Arches, a sacred place. One finds here spirituality without theological doctrine.

When we enter, our surroundings tell us we are in a sequestered place, apart from the messiness of the outside world. We know what we are going to say, what will be said to us, what we will eat, how it will taste, how much it will cost. Ronald, oh Ronald—what have you done to us?

Such a question is easier to ask than to answer. Language is a powerful, compex tool, like Proteus taking multiple forms, shapes, meanings. Words, like things, change fast. Enter the Era of Fast Foods.

That McDonald's was able to reflect and to shape the innate desires and needs of a generation is widely acknowledged. Ronald's "QSC" (Quality, Service, and Cleanliness) was a kind of QED to the propositions of our time. To have expanded from one restaurant in 1955 to thousands here and abroad validates the "miracle." What is harder to get at is the intangible meaning—the mythic and ironic overtones. What is the inner meaning of Ronald's world? Why is it a powerful spore of popular culture on the American landscape?

The impact of fast foods, on our stomachs and our psyches, has only begun to be realized and reported. *Time* magazine's July 4, 1977, issue featured as cover and commentary "Eating on the Run." The open road has become fast-food alley. It is not our endless plains and purple mountains that the young poeticize now. They reflect a new landscape and poetry:

> Shakey's Pizza, Tastee Freez
> A&W, Hardee's.
>
> Howard Johnson, Red Barn, Blimpie,
> House of Pizza, Big Boy, Wimpy.
>
> Wendy's, Friendly's, Taco Titos,
> Sandy's, Arby's, Los Burritoes.

The giant under the golden arches is McDonald's, who counts sales not in the thousands or millions but in the billions. Fast food is now truly ubiquitous in American life. Even those who want no part of it cannot avoid hearing its advertising, seeing its installations, or smelling its aromas wherever crowds gather to relax or be amused.

The "idea" of Ronald—a clown who has our best interests at

heart and shows us reality behind the world's woes—is an ancient and usable one. The act of genius has been to link him with fast food, to merge the image and idea into an organic concept and a visible artifact: the Big Mac.

Fast foods have been around for centuries. The Romans had one-dish instant service shops all over Rome and their empire. Winning generals have featured fast-food formulas for centuries. The sandwich, a key invention, was the work of an English earl, not an American cook. But if (as Anthelme Brillat-Savarin claimed in 1826), "The destiny of nations depends on the manner in which they nourish themselves," the United States may well be the first nation whose destiny depends on hamburgers and other fast foods. McDonald's improved something American that was already "traditional." We were gulping it down long before Ronald. A century ago, the diner was a railroad car equipped for meals-on-the-go; when the diners stopped rolling, they (and trolley cars) were moved to central spots, and the food kept rolling. During the Depression, fast and cheap food places opened known as "greasy spoons" or "sloppy joes." A touch of elegance was added when a New England ice cream peddler, Howard Johnson, opened a string of orange-roofed "roadside cathedrals" and was awarded in 1940 an exclusive food service contract for the 160-mile Pennsylvania Turnpike. Both the road and the restaurant were safe, smooth, and well graded; Johnson cloned the cone long before McDonald's cloned the clown. A new couplet was heard around the land:

> There's many a king on a gilded throne
> But there's only one king on an ice-cream cone!

Soon other "chains" were opened (Hot Shoppes and Stuckeys), and in the ensuing Age of Affluence, the growth was phenomenal. Fast-food restaurant sales topped $20 billion in 1979, with more than 60,000 franchised units in operation. Scholars of American culture were by then writing not only of folkways but also of foodways as well.[4]

They pointed out that fast foods were not just another way of stuffing food into one's mouth; it involves a process that has to do with a thousand memories of a thousand meals, picnics, ball games, vacations. Eating "on the run" can be, and often is, ritualistic. Eating them with others is a form of communion; we consume not only a burger but a cipher. No wonder the pop artists are fascinated with hamburgers. They are close to the center of contemporary popular culture.

This, I suggest, is why the burger ("ham" gets lost in colloquial speech) has become a major phenomenon of our time, why burger joints spring up on highways, city boulevards, and small-town streets like mushrooms (which they often architecturally resemble). For every dollar spent on food eaten away from home, an estimated forty cents goes to fast-food emporiums. No matter what happens to the economy, the total sales rise.

With that much at stake, there is a lot of competition. Look around you, at the permutations on the basic hamburger, bearing odd, hyped-up names that take time to master, much less understand. But a snack that hits the spot on one day is likely to do so every day, thanks to tight control of quality and portion size by the large chains. Familiarity with fast food does not breed contempt—only profit.

Many find formal restaurants intimidating and expensive. They like in-and-out eateries. No snooty headwaiters, no discomfort over which fork to use; the teenagers who take your order at the counter are just like the ones next door or on magazine covers, billboards, and television screens. Eli Whitney, take heart; American kids munching tasty burgers have become interchangeable parts. Ronald is happy with his world.

Before Ronald came Ray—Ray Albert Kroc, born in 1902 of Slavic parents on Chicago's West Side. If the hamburger is the real hero of our true-to-life drama, then Ray is at its proverbial right hand, stopwatch clicking. Although there is no indication of a close friendship, Kroc served with Walt Disney as a Red Cross ambulance driver in World War I. Having tried several other jobs, Kroc settled down in 1923 as a salesman of paper cups for Lily-Tulip. In 1941, he got franchise rights for a new milkshake-mixer, and started Prince Castle Sales Division. This was eight years before Richard and Maurice McDonald opened up a hamburger stand in San Bernardino, California.

By concentrating on burgers and fries, served in disposable wrappers, and by reducing the ordering process to a simple code, the McDonald brothers developed an assembly line that could deliver food quickly and cheaply. Specialization, efficiency, uniformity, and volume had been sacred for American industry since Henry Ford turned out his first Model T, but as Kroc the veteran salesman sat beneath the golden arches in the California sun in 1953, watching the endless flow of customers, he realized what was missing. Somebody had to put the show on the road!

Kroc's visit to San Bernardino is called "the historic three days," during which he "discovered" McDonald's. The miracle begins to unfold:

1955—Kroc's first McDonald's franchise opens in Des Plaines, Illinois.
1956—With a total net worth of $90,000, Kroc borrows $1.5 million.
1961—For $2.9 million Kroc buys all rights to the McDonald's concept from the California brothers.
1963—Major menu innovation: double burger and double cheeseburger.
1964—Number of outlets for McDonald's more than double that of 1960; now 570.
1965—McDonald's goes public.
1966—McDonald's becomes a national name; Ronald goes on national network.
1967—The end of the era of the fifteen cent hamburger. Inflation forces price up to eighteen cents; the beginning of Ronald's role as "official spokesman."
1968—New company architecture: red-and-white tile gives way to more lavish, complex world. Big Mac introduced. Ronald clowns his way into national mythology.

The mechanized hamburger was Kroc's mission and Ronald's world: bright, happy, clean, bedecked with Ronald McDonald goodies and glasses. Promotional campaigns give children free hamburgers and soft drinks on their birthdays. Dispensers of napkins and straws are placed in the customer area, allowing youngsters to do things for themselves. Mothers, who make most meal decisions, endorse their children's preferences. The food is economical, fast, quality-controlled, appealing.

These adjectives have been supported by actual analysis, and calorie counts, by Maryellen Spencer for an article called "Can Mama Mac Get Them to Eat Spinach?"[5] Based on laboratory analysis, tests proved that McDonald's not only meets prescribed government standards, it surpasses them.

Advertising slogans like "You deserve a break today" and "We do it all for you" enticed the working mother. Aware of McDonald's family appeal, Kroc will not permit his restaurants to become "hangouts." "We don't allow cigarette machines, newspaper racks, not even a pay telephone. We made the hamburger joint a dignified, clean place with a wholesome atmosphere."

His restaurants often share a similar architectural design, supporting findings that chains which standardize their appearance cultivate a "family" image that subconsciously appeals to Americans through a process of identification. Restaurants are characterized by the golden arches, an American flag, and a sign that proclaims how many hamburgers have been sold. Standardized stores, with flags stressing patriotism, appeal to middle-class Americans, who comprise the greatest percentage of consumers.

Kroc identifies with these people—like Ronald, he wants to be a father to millions of hungry American kids. Customers are "my people," the company "my baby." He likes to refer to himself as "The Hamburger Man." Fiercely competitive, he favors laissez-faire economics and declares that anyone who wants the consumer's eating-out dollar is his competitor. A 1976 book by Max Boas and Steve Chain, *Big Mac: The Unauthorized Story of McDonald's,* pictured a ruthless mentality and policy—but the billions of hamburgers kept rolling off the line.

That others were more appreciative of Ray Kroc's efforts is attested by the fact that in 1971 he received the annual Good Scout Award from the Boy Scouts of America. Kroc's own idea of a good scout was Richard Nixon, to whose campaigns he gave generously. Now, it seems, he has switched his admiration to Ronald Reagan.

As Reagan once did, Kroc continues to live "the good life" on his California ranch. To a reporter from *Institutions* magazine, June 1978, he gave these details:

I have 22 twin bed rooms, each with private bath and I have semi-
nars out there. I don't know whether you've seen the Big Mac
bus? Well, I bought one for an experiment here in Chicago. I
bought a 40-foot Greyhound bus and had it customized. It cost
$150,000, carries 17. It's absolutely beautiful inside. It's like a
yacht on wheels. I have a shower and a bathroom, a galley and a
bar. Television, telephone. And a make-up table if the gal wants to
make-up or something. I have the logo on the side and the back of
the bus. And I have a 72-foot boat.

The man who has accomplished these things—an electronic
Horatio Alger—is too clever to let the clown or the places in
which Ronald cavorts remain static. He has been quick to cope
with minorities, ethnic groups, women's movements, nostalgia,
regionalism. Ronald is selling a standardized, mass-produced
product, but he is selling magic too. That is his secret weapon.

"When you're in this business," says Ronald's master, Kroc,
"you're in show business. Every day is a new show. It's like a
Broadway musical. IF they hum your tune, you're a success."

Ronald has them humming; not only in America, but all over
the world. The idea of Ronald is contagious. There are dozens of
American hamburgers. The Everywhere Community is becoming international—not just as global communication and shared
information, but as identical products and processes. National
boundaries, and separate words, merge:

TWOALLBEEFPATTIESSPECIALSAUCELETTUCE
CHEESEPICKLESONIONSONASESAMESEEDBUN

But the battle is far from won. By 1980, a host of competitors
had appeared, and McDonald's announced a new companywide
policy known as "seize restaurant superiority." Paul Schrage,
executive vice-president of marketing, predicted a "shakeout of
weaker, less aggressive fast food companies" in the days ahead.[6]

The new campaign managed by the same agency that gave us
Ronald (Needham, Harper, and Steers) was ready with an original
song and different words for the old claim:

Nobody can do it like McDonald's can.
Nobody, nobody else in this whole land . . .
You're the reason we do it
Nobody can do it like McDonald's can.

In addition to major print ads, McDonald's saturated the radio, running the gamut from country and western to disco, featuring the voices of Tammy Wynette, Gloria Gaynor, Rose Royce, Paul Anka, and Seals and Crofts. The annual ad and promotion budget was set at around $200 million. That's a lot of money to sell a lot of beef.

Behind Big Mac stands the mass-produced car that produced the endless highways, roadside stops, gas stations, and honky-tonks. All this took shape during the Great Depression, although segments of it appeared even earlier. Drugstores gave way to drive-ins, which flourished first in the South, where year-round operation was easy. As early as 1921, R. W. Jackson's "Pig Stand" did well on the Dallas-Fort Worth highway; by 1938, there were forty-five "Pig Stands." Few scholars or historians took them seriously then—just as few take McDonald's seriously forty years later. I have tried to take fast foods seriously and to make it clear *why*. If McDonald's is a cultural microcosm, we must study it carefully. Only then can we understand the macrocosm.

Consider three arches: Virginia's Natural Bridge (of stone), St. Louis's Memorial Arch (of steel), McDonald's golden arch (of neon lights and glass). The first celebrated a natural God, the second an industrial frontier, the third a mechanized American dream. That is why we clone clowns.

NOTES

1. See Marian Murray, *Circus! From Rome to Ringling* (Westport, Conn.: Greenwood Press, 1973), chapter 2.
2. There is a fascinating body of literature on fools and clowns. A

cornerstone is Carl Flogel's *Geschiche der Hofnarren,* first published at Leipzig in 1789, and reprinted in New York by Siegert, Liegnitz, and Leitzig in 1977. In this century, key works are Allardyce Nicol, *Masks, Mimes, and Miracles* (New York: Cooper Square, 1931); Mircea Eliade, *Images and Symbols* (New York: Andrews and McNeel, 1961); Tristan Remy, *Clownnummern* (Cologne: Kiepenheur und Witsch, 1964); William Willefore, *The Fool and His Sceptor* (Evanston, Ill.: Northwestern University Press, 1969); and Harvey Cox, *Feast of Fools* (New York: Harper & Row, 1970).

3. Letter to the author from Ms. Cindy Williams, administrative coordinator, McDonald's Corporation, dated July 19, 1977.

4. Starting in 1968, McDonald Corporation's public affairs staff sponsored annual "Awareness Studies" for make-believe characters. The fourth, conducted in 1971, showed that 96 percent of American children could identify Ronald by name, making him a close second to Santa Claus. Has our clown overtaken the reindeer by now?

5. Her article appears in *The World of Ronald McDonald* (Bowling Green, Ohio: Popular Press, 1977), edited by Marshall W. Fishwick.

6. See *Advertising Age,* April 23, 1979, p. 94.

FURTHER READING

Boas, Max, and Chain, Steve. *Big Mac: The Unauthorized Story of McDonald's* (New York: E. P. Dutton, 1976).

Disher, Maurice W. *Clowns and Pantomimes* (New York: Macmillan, 1925).

Fishwick, Marshall, ed. *The World of Ronald McDonald* (Bowling Green, Ohio: Popular Press, 1978).

Kroc, Ray. *Grinding It Out: The Making of McDonald's* (Chicago: Henry Regnery Co., 1977).

Nouwen, Henri. *Clowning in Rome* (New York: Doubleday Image, 1979).

17
COMMON FUTURE

O brave new world!

William Shakespeare

Shakespeare himself would have gloried in it—the royal wedding of Prince Charles and Lady Diana Spencer, on July 29, 1981—with the great globe itself as their stage.

Not that London stage that Will knew as "his" Globe Theater, but planet earth, around which satellites spun transmitting the image to over 800,000,000 people—one sixth of all humanity. It was a multi-million dollar spectacular, giving us a magnificent image of ourselves—only better.

Perhaps the Great Bard himself, no stranger to royal doings, would have been too awed to report. (Alas, the hundreds of journalists and commentators who *did* were not up to Shakespeare's standards.) How can we explain the interest in and impact of that event, so traditional and antique in setting and meaning? Why did people who have rejected all notions of monarchy and traditional pageantry watch with such fascination?

This book has been an effort to answer that question, and to suggest that just as we have a common past, we have a common future.

I sing a song of cycles. Assuming various shapes and rhythms, dimly perceived and seldom understood, they may involve all the cosmos or one atomic particle . . . a millennium or a moment. Night follows day, spring follows winter, epoch gives way to epoch. In our end is our beginning. Facing death, we rejoice in resurrection.

No new idea, this resurrection. Half the human race (including Hindus and Buddhists) believe in some form of reincarnation. Historian Arnold Toynbee and poet William Butler Yeats have worked out complex cyclical schemes in our own time. What is yet to be done is to apply these grand triumphant visions to gritty, trivial popular culture. What has to be explored is the way in which the past illuminates the present and accelerates what we call (for want of a better word) the future.

We need a new way to deal with what is variously called common/popular/mass/electronic culture, a plan to relate multiple pieces and disparate elements, some of which this book has sought to isolate and analyze.

Specifically, we might apply the concept of cycles and patterns to fads (measured on the annual calendar), trends (longer, but measurable in a single lifetime), movements (overlapping generations), and epochs (moving over centuries). To do any of this, we cannot escape a basic question: HOW CAN WE MEASURE DURATION?

The shape of culture (common or otherwise) depends on the interpretation of time. The way things occupy time seems as varied as are the ways they occupy space. Clocks give only superficial help—metaphors go deeper. The *tempo factor* is critical. It regulates the cycles we seek to unravel.

Two significant velocities for "how things go" seem clear: slow happenings (in small and isolated societies, where no conscious intervention alters the rate of change) and fast happenings (when man and his technology intervene). There are in nature no periodic elements, no types and species of time—only solar time, with no theory of temporal structure.[1]

Our main measuring unit, the century, has no natural rhythm of happening whatsoever. The decade is only a decimal position in the century. Both are arbitrary intervals. What we call historical "periods" or "cycles" are neither necessary nor self-evident. So we cannot hope to prove or predict them by any scheme yet discovered. Even the idea of a generation alters with dramatic increases in our life span. We face changing relations, passing moments, and changing definitions of duration.

The popularity of science fiction and intergalactic space has changed the parameters of the time-duration argument. It is speculated that there have been about 15 *billion* years of cosmic evolution; a universe so old and vast that human affairs at first seem of little consequence. This is stressed by Carl Sagan, America's Number One Celebrity Scientist, who embellishes best-selling books and popular television series with florid cosmic romanticism. (We are "starstuff pondering the stars . . . organized assemblages of ten billion billion billion atoms considering the evolution of atoms.") To envision this evolution on a calendar, beginning on January 1 with the "Big Bang," note that what humans call "history" only occupies the last few seconds of December 31!

Have there been, in this long span, a series of cycles—of deaths and rebirths? Seeking clues, Sagan turns to Hinduism, "the only religion in which the time scales correspond to those of modern scientific cosmology." His answer is a resounding *yes*. Hindu cycles are as short as one calendar day and night—or as long as a day and night of Brahma, 8.64 *billion* years. Even this staggering figure, longer than the age of our earth and its sun, may not be the ultimate one: "There are much longer time scales still."[2]

Yet a student of the American culture in which Sagan's *Cosmos* was a best-seller might well say that the crucial cycle is thirty seconds—the length of most television commercials. Simultaneously, another book—less popular but as perceptive—appeared. It is called *Thirty Seconds,* and in it, author Michael Arlen described in meticulous detail the making of a single short AT&T commercial for long-distance telephone calls.[3] Drawing from scores of participants (planners, promoters, clients, actors, producers), he shows how two years of talk, millions of dollars, countless kilowatts of creative energy, months of intensive filming, and over 10,000 feet of film went into that half-minute product. Do such commercials take us right to the beating heart of today's common culture?

What *keeps* that heart beating, however one measures the cycles? Jacob Bronowski suggests an answer in another optimistic and wide-ranging popular book, *The Ascent of Man.* The secret is faith in and understanding of mankind. Personal commitment of people (or disciplines or institutions) has made the precarious ascent possible and the leadership of Western man undeniable. The real threat is not loss of *jobs* but loss of *nerve.* If we in the West reach out and embrace all the world that lies about us, perhaps we shall maintain that leadership. That "reaching out," in the terms of this book, means reaffirming a common culture, furthering the Great Tradition.

And what a great tradition it is! If we have trouble naming six great authors of today, we can quickly name six for tomorrow: Homer, Dante, Shakespeare, Cervantes, Yeats, and Faulkner. They are beyond our fads and follies. They are a part of our tradition.

We wish that we had more such giants and that they were known to more people. That we lack common denominators and find it hard to specify the structure of common-sense meanings in everyday life are serious and disturbing facts.[4] Has mass culture become an industry that processes, packages, and distributes ads, images, and symbols? As we get more and more technology, are we leaving less and less to the imagination? How can we develop a model that lets us observe and transform the real world into relevant data?

Answers to such perplexing questions are difficult to find, but we know we can understand today only by studying yesterday. Cycles count. Beowulf reappears as Batman.[5] Fallen angels from Milton's *Paradise Lost* reappear in *Star Wars,* carrying laser guns.

President Reagan favors many of the policies (and chose to duplicate the decor of the Inaugural Ball) of President McKinley.

Our cyclical speculation can, with validity, deal with centuries as well as decades. Consider the three major phases of human communication—aural, print, and electronic. In the first nonliterate era, people lived in collective mythic interaction with both tribe and natural environments. The second, beginning with pictograph, ideogram, and hieroglyph, grew into phonetic writing. That cycle led to the first modern mass production of communications, the printing press. The third reversed print's exclusive focus on the eye and individual, recovering the aural inclusive modes from earlier times. In addition to the circular movement involved, we can find common themes or devices that never disappeared. At this point, we need to incorporate the insights of Carl Jung concerning *archetypes*—original models from which all subsequent things of the same type are fashioned.

A good example is the Shadow—a character who appears with but is the opposite of the hero. A typical form is the hostile brother (Cain and Abel); another is the double *(doppelgänger)*. The Shadow archetype stretches back to the ancient Egyptian god Osiris (who contended with hostile brother Set) and comes up to contemporary Hollywood movies like *Duel in the Sun* or Kung Fu sagas in comics, television, and film. Another archetype is the Temptress. Ulysses faced the enchantress Circe, who could transform men into swine. The sirens Rusalka and Lorelei lured many an innocent sailor to a watery grave; centuries later, John Keats's knight fell under the terrible spell of "La Belle Dame sans Merci" ("The Beautiful Lady without Pity").

In the 1970s, rock fans could hear the same story—in a very different setting, of course—when The Eagles made their highly successful album with the hit tune "Witchy Woman."

Many aspects that the scientific-minded thought had gone forever—astrology, the occult, witchcraft, primitivism, shamanism —have cropped up in the most "advanced" societies. The rational West has turned to the ancient mystical East for new insights and systems.

During these astonishing reversions, the United States celebrated its bicentennial in 1976. Abraham Lincoln's words, spoken over a century earlier, were reaffirmed: "There is both a power and a magic in common opinion." The sense of excitement, joy, hope gripped the land. A fleet of sailing ships, the largest assembled since the Spanish Armada, entered New York harbor, reviving a glorious past. We remembered that ours was the oldest continuously functioning written constitution and that we had weathered every storm encountered. We could face the future with optimism. Laurence Peter's popular book, *The Peter Plan,* presented "a blueprint for a better 1990 that is the antithesis of Orwell's *1984.*" Herman Kahn's *The Next Two Hundred Years* was as "a challenge to the doomsday-sayers." William I. Thompson's *Evil and World Order* championed "the qualitative rather than the quantitative humanistic approach" to planetary management. Buckminster Fuller promised better things for better living through geodesic domes. As we liked to say when Franklin Roosevelt followed Herbert Hoover: "Happy Days Are Here Again!"

Further proof of the new optimism came in a national survey of the arts made by the *New York Times.* "Two hundred years is a decent point at which to reassess, even to reconnoiter, the American art scene," Clive Barnes pointed out. "What seemed remarkable about almost all the replies was their spirit of optimism."

Reports on dance, music, and theater bordered on the euphoric. Publishers' lists and profits were increasing. American painting and sculpture continued to be the single most significant contribution to world culture since the end of World War II.

Jimmy Carter chose to walk down Pennsylvania Avenue when he was inaugurated as president. During his presidency, the euphoria disappeared. Crisis after crisis swept over the country. In 1980, a man almost seventy years old was elected by a landslide on a conservative ticket, with the support of fundamental religious groups. Ronald Reagan took office in circumstances remarkably like those of Franklin D. Roosevelt half a century earlier. Was the cycle evident?

If so, what did this say about the American belief in progress? Are we still committed to getting better and better day by day in every way? Is not our chief product progress? Did we get better things for better living through chemistry? Or have we moved from progress to perplexity (as the philosopher-theologian Reinhold Niebuhr suggested)?

No one could deny that changes were accelerating. Might they be more extrinsic than intrinsic? True enough, the speed of a message carried from voice to ear through the medium of air travels at 1,130 feet per second. Sound transmitted by radio waves and electricity moves at 186,000 miles per second—nearly a million times faster, but this does not mean the message is a million times more important or enduring. We recall Thoreau's wry question when told that a telegraph line might be constructed from Texas to Massachusetts. Are we sure, he asked, that the people in Texas have anything to tell us?

Communications "specialists" are fond of accumulating verbs that dramatize what the new technology is doing. But do they draw the right conclusions from the external evidence? Consider this one by Tony Schwartz, a professor of auditory perception who has (his publisher notes) "created more than 5,000 radio and TV spots":

> The world is thus electronically fractured, recorded, transmitted, received, and reassembled in the human brain. The *now* generation is thus a product of the *now* perception.[6]

How does any mere mortal (even one who professes auditory perception) know how my brain "reassembles" information? Is the world any more "fractured" for me than it was for Vincent van Gogh or Cicero? How can any generation or perception endure in the *now* except by emerging from the *then*?

What about the areas that are thrust from an ancient aural *then* into the crackling electronic *now* too fast for psychic or social adjustment? How can they fit new forms into old patterns, without endangering values they hold sacred?

The question surfaced when I hurried down the streets of Colombo, capital of Sri Lanka, in a heavy rainstorm. The city was abandoned, except for a group of youths that (without any raincoats or protection) stood in front of a store window laughing and clapping. "What is going on?" I wondered and walked over to take a look. Inside that store window was a television set. An episode from *Sesame Street* was being aired.

Our goal, as Western powers with huge media resources, should not be to inundate but to revitalize cultural resources around the world. Says John F. Cady after years of studying Southeast Asia:

> We must recognize and augment other people's long-civilized past. The validity of their experiences and their genius for self-expression may contribute alternatives to an outside modernized world committed to material possessions and the exercise of power.[7]

I ponder these words as my jet plane leaves the United States, bound for Asia. First I must go to Hawaii. As we rise far above the world, the world is very much with us. Slim-legged tight-skirted stewardesses come and go, their teeth white and their smiles sculptured. A male voice comes from the intercom:

> Howdy folks! I'm Kennie, your flight purser. Welcome aboard! Gee, it's *fun* to be flying to sunny Hawaii with all of you today. Aloha, as they say on Waikiki. We'll do everything in our power to make this your best trip ever. Just ring if you want us. I can make plane reservations right on board. Our computers never stop. During the flight I'll be in the aisles. I wear a bright red coat and a name tag with KENNIE on it. So sit back and relax. . . .

No thank you. I want to stand up and question. Will we get nothing but a series of fun flying days and bright red coats out of our newly emerging world? Codified, computerized, and televized, what will be our pains, our prospects, our common future?

One thought comes quickly to mind: we'll have to approach all this not as cannon balls but as rubber balls. The cannon ball shatters and levels everything in its path. The rubber ball moves until reaching something hard. Then it bounces back. Bouncing has resilience, humor, perspective. Winnie the Pooh knew this and paid Tigger a compliment:

> Whatever his weight in pounds, shillings, and ounces
> He always seems bigger because of his bounces.

Our hope lies with our bounceability. We have bounced back many times before, and we shall bounce back again. On that we base the case for renewal.

We shall bounce at speeds that Tigger could never have imagined. Speed need not destroy substance. The elements we have examined—tradition, myth, lore, land, dreams, style, process—endure. *Now* contains all past, including the most primal and primitive modes. We must fight to preserve and remythologize the past. Without it, we have no viable future.

We live in a plural present—like every other society that has ever existed. We can study what has been and speculate about what will be; everything varies with time and place. The world alters as we walk in it. Time passes, relations shift, shadows lengthen. We are travelers passing through all too quickly. We want our visit to be full of meaning. That is why we crave a common culture.

The future of that common culture rests in the past: in prehistoric memories, eternal truths, unending struggles. Powerful "facts" have attacked, split, and degraded it, but rebirth and renewal are under way. The world is wired for sight and sound, the old barriers are crumbling. A new renaissance is at hand.

Many perils await us. The same rocket boosters that could carry probes to other planets could carry nuclear bombs to other nations—one road marks discovery, the other destruction. On the one road, a greater tradition than we have yet imagined may emerge. All the elements of a new mythology return, rejuvenated. Now it is up to us.

NOTES

1. George Kubler, *The Shape of Time* (New Haven: Yale University Press, 1962), chapter 4.
2. Carl Sagan, *Cosmos* (New York: Random House, 1980), p. 258.

3. Michael J. Arlen, *Thirty Seconds* (New York: Penguin, 1981).

4. Aaron Cicourel, *Method and Measurement in Sociology* (Glencoe, Ill.: Free Press, 1964), p. 81.

5. This idea is further elaborated by Roger B. Rollin, "Beowulf to Batman: The Epic Hero and Pop Culture," in *College English* 31:3 (February 1970).

6. Tony Schwartz, *The Responsive Chord* (New York: Anchor, 1972), p. 159.

7. John F. Cady, *The History of Postwar Southeast Asia* (Athens: Ohio University, 1974), p. 699.

FURTHER READING

Eco, Umberto. *A Theory of Semiotics* (Bloomington: University of Indiana Press, 1976).

Lundberg, Louis B. *Future Without Shock* (New York: Norton, 1975).

Pettit, Charles. *The Concept of Structuralism* (Berkeley: University of California Press, 1975).

Toffler, Alvin. *Future Shock* (New York: Macmillan, 1970), and *The Eco-Spasm Report* (New York: Bantam, 1975).

Vacca, Roberto. *The Coming Dark Age* (New York: Doubleday, 1975).

Ward, Barbara. *Spaceship Earth* (New York: Harper & Row, 1964).

ANNOTATED
BIBLIOGRAPHY

UNCOMMON PLEASURE awaits those who test the words of this book in the places where they apply: the marketplace, mall, movie house, stadium, rally, riot, and convention.

Others will prefer to continue their reading—available sources are everywhere (newspapers, posters, books, magazines, almanacs, journals, etc.). For the scholar, there is the printed *Abstracts of Popular Culture,* which scans over 900 magazines. Among the many publications of major importance to the study of common culture are *American Quarterly, American Historical Review, American Studies International, Journal of American Culture, Journal of Popular Culture, Humanities in Society, Isis, Minerva, Technology and Culture, International Popular Culture,* and *Journal of Regional Cultures.*

The short annotated bibliography that follows might start you in new directions. The journey is endless and endlessly exciting. Good luck!

Allen, Don. *The Electric Humanities: Patterns for Teaching Mass Media and Popular Culture* (Los Angeles: Pflaum, 1971).
Allen attempts to expand the traditional view of humanistic study and scholarship, arguing for the inclusion of popular literature, theater, and music. He believes we must teach and learn in "the total environment."

Berger, Arthur Asa. *The Comic-Stripped American* (Baltimore: Penguin Books, Inc., 1974).
A zany look at culture as revealed through comics—the collective daydream of the American imagination.

_____. *Pop Culture* (Dayton: Pflaum/Standard, 1973).
A provocative survey of amusements and entertainments; common objects and everyday activities; styles, symbols, and social phenomena.

Bernstein, Jeremy. *Hans Bethe: Prophet of Energy* (New York: Basic Books, 1980).
A leading physicist writes a "popular" book about a complex scientist (as he did with his 1973 biography of *Einstein*). Bethe was a German-born scientist who helped develop the atom bomb and then worked to restrict its use. See also Bernstein's *Experiencing Science* (New York: Basic Books, 1978).

Bigsby, C.W.E. *Superculture: American Popular Culture and Europe* (Bowling Green, Ohio: Popular Press, 1975).
A selection of essays on how American popular culture changes in both meaning and structure when it is carried abroad.

_____. *Approaches to Popular Culture* (Bowling Green, Ohio: Popular Press, 1976).
An anthology of seventeen essays under the headings of "Perspectives," "Images," and "Examinations." Especially valuable for material on Marxism.

Blalock, Herbert. *An Introduction to Social Research* (Englewood Cliffs, N.J.: Prentice Hall, 1970).
What is research methodology all about? What can it tell us of man, media, and society?

Boorstin, Daniel J. *The Image: A Guide to Pseudo-Events in America* (New York: Harper Colophon, 1964).

Welcome to the image-making world of pseudo-events in the news—the world of celebrities, tourists, and big business public relations gimmicks.

Browne, Ray B. *Rituals and Ceremonies in Popular Culture* (Bowling Green, Ohio: Popular Press, 1980).

A wide-ranging collection of essays dealing with such subjects as prom queens, cockfights, funerals, pornography, and ritual killing in Vietnam.

————, and Ambrosetti, R. J. *Popular Culture and Curricula* (Bowling Green, Ohio: Popular Press, 1970).

A survey of popular culture courses in universities and high schools at the beginning of the 1970s. Although the emphasis and content have changed considerably since then, this study documents the enormous impact of the 1960s on the field.

————, and Fishwick, Marshall W. *Icons of America* (Bowling Green, Ohio: Popular Press, 1978).

This anthology attempts to define the "iconic" quality of everyday things, relate them to iconic history, and show how Coke bottles, postage stamps, television sets, blue jeans, and lp records fulfill ancient functions in the modern world.

Burke, Peter. *Popular Culture in Early Modern Europe* (New York: Harper & Row, 1978).

An important and original study that attempts to describe and interpret the popular culture of Europe between 1500 and 1800; worthy of close attention.

Calas, Nicholas, and Calas, Elena. *Icons and Images of the Sixties* (New York: E. P. Dutton, 1971).

An analysis of the chief styles and developments in American art in the 1960s, arguing forcefully for the ethical basis of art.

Cannel, Ward, and Macklin, June. *The Human Nature Industry* (New York: Anchor, 1973).

What we call "human nature," these authors contend, is put together, distributed through mass communication, advertised by experts, and ultimately consumed by humans. Humor and horror in such an interpretation are both signs of our time.

Cantor, Norman F., and Werthman, Michael S., eds. *The History of Popular Culture* (New York: Macmillan, 1968).
One of the most important anthologies yet produced, this book attempts to describe popular culture from ancient times to the present. Lack of criteria and standards limit its usefulness, but it still provides a scope not found often.

Cawelti, John G. *The Six-Gun Mystique* (Bowling Green, Ohio: Popular Press, 1971).
Carefully chosen selection of essays to reveal the dimension, subjects, and art of the study of an American artifact.

_____. *Adventure, Mystery, and Romance: Formula Stories as Art* (Chicago: University of Chicago Press, 1976).
The first general theory for the analysis of popular literary formulas and for the fantasy world of danger, mystery, and excitement. The book is a model of careful research and theory building.

Deer, Irving, and Deer, Harriet A. *The Popular Arts: A Critical Reader* (New York: Charles Scribner's Sons, 1967).
Informative essays by various critics who explore the "worth of the values reflected in the popular arts, the kinds of tastes and attitudes reflected, and the meaning implied by enjoyment of the popular arts."

Dolan, Paul J., and Quinn, Edward. *Sense of the 70's* (New York: Oxford University Press, 1978).
A well-wrought reader that captures the shape and substance of a mixed and controversial decade. The "Me Decade" gets a close and revealing look.

Ferguson, Marilyn. *The Aquarian Conspiracy: Personal and Social Transformation in the 1908s* (Los Angeles: J. P. Tarcher, 1980).
An effort to explain the "great shuddering irrevocable shift" that is overtaking us, transforming all institutions, and moving us into the Age of Aquarius—a millenium of love and light.

Fishwick, Marshall, ed. *The World of Ronald McDonald* (Bowling Green, Ohio: Popular Press, 1978).
Ronald as symbol and key to the vast McDonald empire, which has influenced not only our eating but also our decor, mythology, and ethnography.

_____. *Parameters of Popular Culture* (Bowling Green, Ohio: Popular Press, 1974).

In this excursion through contemporary society, the author attends to heroes, celebrities, icons, fakelore, theology, and art in an effort to delineate the form and value of our "way of life."

_____. *The Hero American Style* (New York: David McKay Co., 1969).
"Heroes are mirrors of the times. . . . Heroes (pro, anti-, non) rise and fall too quickly for analysis . . . life styles change . . . but heroes never go out of style. Myths shape the man; style shows how it has shaped him."

Friendly, Fred W. *Due to Circumstances Beyond Our Control* (New York: Random House, 1967).
Provocative and disquieting view of the networks by an insider. "Doubtless there is more in these pages about me than anyone cares to know, but I propose to tell the trials of broadcast journalism by sharing my sixteen-year experience at CBS. . . ."

Gowans, Alan. *The Unchanging Arts* (Philadelphia: J. B. Lippincott Co., 1971).
Study of the interrelationship between popular and elite arts. Gowans' thesis is that the only arts that are alive and continue to live are those that are born in and continue to serve utilitarian needs. The other arts are dead. "Past generations did not live their lives with remote posterity in mind."

Grunig, James. *Decline of the Global Village* (New York: General Hall, 1976).
A strong attack on Marshall McLuhan and his school and a quantitative analysis of how specialization is changing the mass media.

Halberstam, David. "CBS: The Power and the Profits." *The Atlantic,* January and February 1976, pp. 33ff. and 52ff.
A critical analysis of the executive suite at CBS, although mostly about its news practices and policies.

Hirsch, Paul M. "Processing Fads and Fashion: An Organization-set Analysis of Cultural Industry Systems." *American Journal of Sociology,* January 1972, pp. 639–59.
A sociological analysis of the mass media as forming a general type of industrial organization, comparing the media to other industries that sell "fads and fashions."

Hopkins, Jerry. *The Rock Story* (New York: New American Library, Signet, 1970).

"The story of Rock from the inside, the story the fan mags won't-or-can't-tell. The stars, the groupies, the gossip, the promo, the hype, and the big sound itself."

Jacobs, Norman, ed. *Culture for the Millions? Mass Media in Modern Society* (Princeton: D. Van Nostrand, 1961).
Collection of essays by various contributors. Analysis of the differences between those forms of expression communicated by the mass media and other popular varieties of art. Reading these essays shows how rapidly our culture has evolved, at least superficially, in the last twenty years.

Kolker, Robert P. *A Cinema of Loneliness* (New York: Oxford, 1980).
Seeing cinema as "a popular art in conflict," this book focuses on five of the most interesting contemporary directors—Arthur Penn, Stanley Kubrick, Francis Ford Coppola, Martin Scorsese, and Robert Altman. They form the nucleus of what some call "The New Hollywood" and "the American New Wave."

Luedtke, Luther S. *The Study of American Culture: Contemporary Conflicts* (DeLand, Fla.: Everett Edwards, 1977).
To date, the best collection of essays recapitulating the history and dilemma of American Studies. The field is seen as a forum for unresolved struggles in a mass-mediated world. There is an extensive bibliography.

McLuhan, Marshall. *The Mechanical Bride: Folklore of Industrial Man* (New York: The Vanguard Press, 1951).
Here is McLuhan's primer on popular culture assessment, including a series of vignettes on various cultural phenomena such as ads, comics, Tarzan, Emily Post, sports, market research.

_____. *Understanding Media* (New York: McGraw-Hill, 1964).
The works of this author are of the utmost importance. This particular book is most comprehensive. "Rapidly, we approach the final phase of the extension of man—the technological stimulation of consciousness, when the creative process of knowing will be collectively and corporately extended to the whole of human society, much as we have already extended our senses and our nerves by the various media."

_____, with Barrington Nevitt. *Take Today: The Executive as Dropout* (New York: Harcourt Brace Jovanovich, 1972).
A look at the future through the lens of business and management. If one does not take it too seriously, the book helps to point out some of the foibles of "big business."

Mann, Dennis A., ed. *The Arts in a Democratic Society* (Bowling Green, Ohio: Popular Press, 1978).
Provocative essays by Alan Gowans, Constance Perin, Willis Truitt, John A. Kouwenhoven, Herbert A. Gans, Leslie Fiedler, and Dennis Mann.

Nachbar, Jack, Weiser, Deborah, and Wright, John L. *The Culture Reader* (Bowling Green, Ohio: Popular Press, 1978).
One of a series of monographs and readers, concentrating on myths, icons, stereotypes, heroes, rituals, and formulas.

Newcomb, Horace. *TV: The Most Popular Art* (New York: Anchor Press/ Doubleday, 1974).
A book of wide scope that goes beyond the peripheral question and puts television into a wide cultural perspective. This book would be particularly valuable for a beginning class.

———. *Television: The Critical View* (New York: Oxford University Press, 1976).
Divided into three parts ("Seeing Television," "Thinking about Television," and "Defining Television"), this book contains the most articulate and literate essays yet brought together in a single anthology.

Nye, Russel B. *The Unembarrassed Muse: The Popular Arts in America* (New York: The Dial Press, 1970).
By far the most comprehensive single study of the various aspects of popular culture in America. Standard and required reading. Extensive bibliography.

Oganov, Grigori. *Genuine Culture and False Substitutes* (Moscow: Novosti Press, 1979).
Socialist culture is "genuine," that of capitalism—especially the popular aspects—"false." The standard Marxist ideology applied to various aspects of popular culture, centering on Lenin's famous dictum: "One cannot live in society and be free from society." Important insights for non-Marxist scholars.

Parks, Gordon. *Born Black* (Philadelphia: J. P. Lippincott, 1971).
A "personal report on the decade of black revolt, 1960–1970" by a black man at ease with himself and with the white world, this short book has great wisdom and merit.

Rosenberg, Bernard, with David Manning White. *Mass Culture: The Popular Arts in America* (Boston: The Free Press, 1957).

This collection of forty-nine essays is prefaced by two excellent pieces: one by Rosenberg is a radical critique of mass culture and the other by David Manning White is a defense of it. A variety of other intellectuals comment on movies, literature, television, advertising, and popular music.

Sagan, Carl. *Cosmos* (New York: Random House, 1980).

Both the book and the television program of the same name have achieved unprecedented popularity. The author, a distinguished academic, tries to explain the cosmos with lucid language and flights into florid romanticism. When the title became the Book-of-the-Month, journalists promptly branded Sagan "America's Number One Celebrity Scientist."

Schechter, Harold, and Semeiks, J. G. *Patterns in Popular Culture: A Sourcebook for Writers* (New York: Harper & Row, 1980).

Eight chapters are devoted to a single archetypal or mythic pattern: The Shadow, The Trickster, The Temptress, The Mother, The Wise Old Man, The Helpful Animal, The Quest, and The Rebirth. Many of the selections go far back into history, giving the text a wide scope.

Schramm, Wilbur, and Roberts, Donald. *The Process and Effects of Mass Communication* (Urbana: University of Illinois Press, 1971).

The beginning guide to communications research. See especially Schramm's essay for a theoretical overview.

Schroeder, Fred E. H. *Outlaw Aesthetics* (Bowling Green, Ohio: Popular Press, 1978).

The author argues that we must not damn popular art because it does not fit elite standards, but try instead to develop sensitive new ones, standards that are long overdue.

Sklar, Robert. *Movie-Made America: A Cultural History of American Movies* (New York: Vintage/Random House, 1976).

This volume attempts not only to present the cultural history of American movies from the 1890s to the present but also "to provide a broad framework for understanding their significance."

Toffler, Alvin. *The Culture Consumers* (New York: Vintage, 1973).

This examination of the arts in relation to the university, business, artists, managers, patrons, and the government says much about the use of leisure time and the nature of culture in America.

Tunstall, Jeremy. *The Media Are American* (New York: Columbia University Press, 1977).
A well-documented account of our media exports and their astonishing —sometimes bizarre—effects on the world. Media imperialism is defined and explored.

Valdes, Joan, with Jeanne Crow. *The Media Reader* (Dayton: Pflaum, 1975).
An anthology of readings on newspapers, magazines, comics, radio, television, movies, and advertising.

Warshaw, Robert. *The Immediate Experience* (New York: Doubleday, 1964).
Striving to "do some justice to the claims both of art and popular culture," Warshaw wrote what is generally considered one of the best books yet done on film criticism.

Whetmore, Edward. *Mediamerica* (Belmont, Calif.: Wadsworth, 1978).
A free-style fun-filled account by a second-generation McLuhanite who packs a lot of material into a small space and finds images to illustrate it.

White, David M. *Pop Culture in America* (Chicago: Quadrangle Books, Inc., 1970).
A comprehensive survey of key areas of popular culture. "The mass media endemically mirror the prevailing social climate, so popular culture over the next quarter-century will be no better or worse than our society demands and therefore deserves."

Wolfe, Tom. *The Right Stuff* (New York: Simon and Schuster, 1979).
All about the astronauts, by the New Journalist who set many of the writing trends of the 1960s. High-style popular writing.

Zinsser, William. *Pop Goes America* (New York: Harper & Row, 1966).
A smorgasbord of witty observations about the pop culture of the 1960s: pop art, Barbie dolls, James Bond, Woody Allen.

INDEX

About the Author

Marshall W. Fishwick is Professor of Humanities and Communications at Virginia Technical University in Blacksburg. He has written many books including: *Popular Architecture, Icons of Popular Culture,* and *A New Map of Learning.*